The Mysterious, Magical Cat

Books of Similar Interest from
RANDOM HOUSE VALUE PUBLISHING

Best Cat Stories
The Cat Lover's Book of Fascinating Facts
Cat Spells
Cat Tales
The Personality of the Cat
Psychic Pets
The World of Cats

THE MYSTERIOUS, MAGICAL CAT

D. J. Conway

Gramercy Books
New York

Calligraphic cat illustrations by Shelly Bartek
Poem on page 10 by Joyce Smith
Stories in Chapter 2 by ShadowCat, Jean Fritz, Cerridwen, S. Shelton, Kimberly Gibbs, Tracy Corpe, Robyn L. Brown, Chameleon Silvercat, Nan Skovran, Dankya Edwards, Delores Wheeler, Lee Prosser, Lynda Lee Macken, Ingrid Gordon, and Jeanne McLarney

Note: The arcane spelling of magickal reflects the author's choice of using ancient and mystical texts to describe esoteric material. The publisher has chosen to use the more modern spelling of magical on the jacket and title page of the book.

This 2000 edition is published by Gramercy Books™, an imprint of Random House Value Publishing, Inc., 280 Park Avenue, New York, N.Y. 10017, by arrangement with Llewellyn Publications, St. Paul, MN

Gramercy Books™ and design are trademarks of Random House Value Publishing, Inc.

Random House
New York • Toronto • London • Sydney • Auckland
http://www.randomhouse.com/

Printed and bound in the United States of America.

Library of Congress Cataloging–in–Publication Data

Conway, D. J. (Deanna J.).
   The mysterious, magical cat / D.J. Conway.
      p. cm.
   Originally published: St. Paul, Minn.: Llewellyn Publications, c1998.
   Includes bibliographical references (p.).
   ISBN 0-517-16301-2
   1. Cats--Folklore. 2. Cats--Mythology. I. Title.

GR725 .C65 2000
133'.2599752--dc21

00-037143

9 8 7 6 5 4 3 2

To all the cats who have graced my life:

Figaro, Muff, Samuel Tibbs, Flash, Gypsy, Finnigan, Callie, Valkyrie, Beowulf, Hocus Pocus, Hexi, and Shadow Boy.

And to all the other little cats in the world.

Contents

Introduction

The Mysterious, Magickal Cat

Few species have evoked such extremes in human emotions as the feline family. For centuries, felines have invoked admiration, awe, inspiration, and fear. Cats are mysterious, mystical creatures who predict earthquakes, volcanic eruptions, and storms through their behavior, react to haunted buildings, and psyche you out by following the movement of things you cannot see. We are fascinated by cats and their behavior, their regal bearing, their intelligence. Yet we are upset by their inscrutable stare and their savage natural instincts.

> Beware of people who dislike cats.
>
> —OLD IRISH PROVERB

Even to confirmed cat lovers, the domesticated cat is a mysterious creature who shares its affections as if conferring a royal honor, scorning attention when it feels insulted yet giving itself to total abandon when enticed to play.

Cats are first and always their own creature. No human can ever truly say he or she owns a cat. As Peter Engel and Merrit Malloy said in their book, dogs obediently come when you order them to, while cats look at you with disinterest, do the equivalent of taking a number and vaguely give the impression of getting back to you at their convenience.[1]

To most people, cats are an animal they either like or dislike. There seem to be few fence sitters on the subject of cats. A cat lover is called an ailurophile, while one who fears or hates cats is called an ailurophobe.

---

1. Peter Engel and Merrit Malloy, *Old Wives' Tales.*

Usually when we speak in general terms of cats, we mean the domesticated cat. However, every single cat of any size belongs to the class Mammalia, the order Carnivora, and the family of Felidae or felids. The cat family includes about thirty-nine species of cat, ranging from tigers to domestic cats.

Unfortunately, history (after the time of the ancient Egyptians and the most well-known of cat goddesses, Bast) and many religions have not been kind to the feline family, especially the smallest of its members—the domesticated cat. Many of the feline family have also been hunted to near extinction. Malicious, superstitious lies have been built around its character and supposedly nefarious deeds.

The English word *cat* has its equivalent in many other cultures. In French it is called *chat*, in German *Katze*, Italian *gatto*, Spanish *gato*, Swedish *katt*, Norwegian *katt*, Dutch *Kat*, Icelandic *kottur*, Polish *kot*, Yiddish *kats*, Greek *gata*, Maltese *qattus*, modern Arabic *qittah*, Nubian *kadiz*, and in fourth-century Latin *cattus*.[2] The Egyptian word for cat was *miu* or *mau*, while in China the word was (and still is) *mao*.

The Turkish word *kedi* (cat) may have been the source of our word *kitty* or *kitten*, just as the word *tabby* may have come from the Turkish word *utabi*. Many believe that the words *puss* and *pussy* came from the names of the Egyptian cat goddesses Pasht and Bast.[3]

The ancestors of the domesticated cat were already well established on our planet when humans appeared 30,000 to 35,000 years ago. The cat family, in one form or another, spread around the globe, with the exceptions of Australia, Antarctica, Madagascar, the West Indies, and some of the oceanic islands.

Excavations of human settlements such as Jericho have produced cat bones dated as early as 9,000 years ago. In 1983, the archaeologist Alain le Brun found feline jawbones and teeth in a Neolithic settlement in south Cyprus, which dated back to 6000 B.C.E.[4] There were no native wild cats on Cyprus, so cats must have been brought to the island by humans. Harappa, in the Indus Valley, yielded cat bones dating back

2. Richard H. Gebhardt, *The Complete Cat Book.*
3. F. E. Zeuner, *A History of Domesticated Animals*, believed that all names for the cat came from the Near East and Africa.
4. Gebhardt, *The Complete Cat Book.*
5. Zeuner, *A History of Domesticated Animals.*

4,000 years. Records indicate that the Egyptians had tamed and were using wild animals since about 2600 B.C.E.[5]

However, other animals, such as the dog, reindeer, goat, and sheep, were domesticated long before the cat decided to live with humankind. Perhaps cats wanted to see if this new species of animal would be worth cultivating as a friend and benefactor.

Cats may have domesticated themselves rather than humans doing the domesticating. When humans began to grow and store grain, the cats may have come into the villages because of the rodent population that fed off the grain. Observing that these cats killed rats and mice, the farmers probably started feeding them in hopes they would stay around and protect the food supply. And cats, seeing the golden opportunity of plenty of food and protection from larger predators, decided to live with humans—but only on their terms.

A cat stalks a rat in this woodcut from an early nineteenth-century spelling book

I sincerely hope that the people of this world who are still suspicious of and hateful to cats will move beyond such actions. After all, how we treat our animal companions says volumes about our true spirituality, or lack of it.

Although I have never had a purebred cat, I have been the custodian of many cats throughout my life: Figaro, Samuel Tibbs, Muff, Gypsy, Flash, Finnigan, Callisto (Callie), Beowulf, Valkyrie, Hocus Pocus, Hexi, and Shadow Boy. I have never failed to be enchanted by members of the feline family, or the tribe of tiger. This book is a tribute to cats and cat lovers everywhere.

SECTION I

The Magickal Cat

Magick of Claw
and Whisker

Cat magick is one of the oldest forms of spellworking among magicians, shamans, and spiritual leaders. Various versions of it were used right up to the times of the witch hunts and cat murders. After that, this type of magick became secret knowledge because of the misconceptions about both cats and magick.

Cats can be cooperative when something feels good, which, to a cat, is the way everything is supposed to feel as much of the time as possible.

—ROGER A. CARAS

The creators of the lies about cats thought to destroy the ancient belief in the sacredness of the feline family, especially the small domestic cat and its ability to help the magician perform magick. They accomplished their goal with a great many humans.

Among magicians and followers of the Old Ways, however, the cat never lost its sacredness. Belief in the cat as co-magician and guide into sacred realms went underground until the danger passed. Today, it is once more safe, at least in the U.S.A. and most European countries, to practice cat magick.

Cat magick absolutely does not use the sacrifice of cats, their blood, or torture of them. Those hideous practices were part of the very system that condemned both cats and magicians, and were never used by the followers of magick and the Old Ways.

Cat magick is a branch of spellworking that can be as lighthearted or serious as the situation demands. It is another method of performing magick, one that can help the magician better understand the flows of energy freely rippling throughout the universe. Cats, like many other animals, are very much aware of these unseen currents of energy and also have strong telepathic connections with humans. Those who hesitate about doing magick because they do not feel comfortable with it may feel more at ease with cat magick, thus opening doors to higher realms of consciousness.

No spells in this book require materials that would be harmfully taken from a cat. In fact, I have set them up in such a way that if the fur, claws, or whiskers are removed from a cat in any cruel manner the spell will not work but will backlash against the magician. Fur can be gathered when brushing or combing the cat, or by removing discarded fur from furniture. Claws also are naturally discarded by cats from time to time; the tips of claws that have been gently cut can also be used. Whiskers, like fur, are shed naturally and can be gathered for spellworking.

Under no circumstances should a magician pull fur or whiskers off a cat or cut the claws more than a tiny amount at the tip. Cutting too much off claws will make them bleed and be sore—think about how you feel when a fingernail breaks down into the quick and bleeds.

Whether you are an advanced magician or a novice, I hope this book about cats and the potential of cat magick will aid you on your upward path of growth.

Elements of Egyptian Magick

The cat is basically a nocturnal creature. In magick, it symbolizes the powers of the night and the Moon. All cultures who had the domestic cat held the belief that the cat is psychic, capable of predicting coming disasters, and wise in the ways of magick. They also agreed that one should be careful about what is said in front of a cat.

Although there were, and are, many cultural branches of magickal workings, many of the basic ideas and methods are very similar.

The Egyptians—of whom we have some of the earliest and most complete records of magick—used two basic, broad categories of magick: one to benefit the living or the dead, and the second to bring harm to others. Thus, Egyptian magicians were trained to deal with both material and spiritual needs. Naturally, there were a few who dabbled in the darker magicks simply because they relished causing harm, but the majority of Egyptians using magick of a questionable nature did so to protect themselves and their families. They must have been quite good at it, for Hebrew, Greek, and Roman writers referred to Egyptian magicians as having great powers and expertise in occult sciences.

In ancient Egypt, images and symbols were used in performing spiritual rituals and magickal spells. Symbols are abstract because they go beyond concrete physical forms. A magician understands that the image and the original are the same, thus the symbol itself has a reality. Egyptian magick was based on the idea that a powerful unseen force,[1] which exists everywhere in the world, can have supernormal effects on people and events if properly used by a magician. Symbols were used as focal points, directing the magician's subconscious mind to higher knowledge and understanding.

Ancient Egyptians revered cats because they believed that the image of a cat, as well as a living cat, would protect against all kinds of evil, both natural and supernatural. Amulets, charms, spells, and words of power pertaining to cats are listed in records of Egyptian magick. A great number of small figures of gods

---

1. This force was called *Hek* or *Hekau* by the Egyptians. The word *Hek* later became the word *hag*, which originally meant a holy sorceress. The word is also connected with the goddess Hecate.

and goddesses, perforated to be worn on a necklace, have been found. Animal figures, particularly that of the cat, were worn on the same necklace.

The word *amulet* comes from an Arabic root word meaning "to bear" or "to carry." Many cultures, besides the Egyptians, used and still use amulets. Amulets are simply various objects and ornaments worn or carried for some kind of protection. Ancient Egyptians often engraved their amulets with *hekau*, or words of power. Engraved figures of scarabs, cats, other animals, and deities were common. These amulets might be of faience, glass,[2] pottery, gold, silver, or semiprecious stones.

A sphinx-inspired piece of ancient Egyptian jewelry

One stone particularly dedicated to the cat throughout much of the Middle East and Egypt was the cat's eye stone. This stone has a shimmer down the middle of it resembling the pupil of a cat's eye. It has long been connected with the belief that it will protect the wearer from evil and death; the Arabs thought it made the wearer invisible.

Staffs topped with the carved heads of sacred animals were carried in processions. Statues were an important part of ritual equipment, for they were symbols of the deity invoked and thus filled with that deity's power. Small ivory wands bearing an engraved cat head have been found buried with the dead.[3]

To the ancient Egyptians, the use of color was very important, not for its eye appeal but for its mystical symbolism. The color red stood for life but it also meant aggression and threats. White meant purity and sanctity; they called it the color of joy. Red and white were considered to be opposites; when used together, they symbolized wholeness and perfection.

Black referred to death and the Underworld, yet it also contained the seeds of rebirth. Blue was a healing color, one that also symbolized the constant flow of infinity. Green symbolized Nature, growing things, and budding life. The ancient Egyptian expression "to do green things" meant to do good things; "to do red things" meant to do evil.

Burning incense was an important part of Egyptian ceremonies, whether public or private. The incense used were gum resins. They believed that incense

2. Glass was a rare, expensive commodity in the ancient world, so prized that pharaohs used it along with gems and gold.
3. E. A. Wallis Budge, *The Liturgy of Funerary Offerings*.

cleansed the person and the area in which the ritual was performed. In fact, the Egyptians called this incense resin "the sweat of the gods."[4]

Bouquets of flowers on the altars represented life. The offering table could be as simple as a woven mat on the floor or a stone table. These mats and tables had sacred symbols on all four corners.

Temples and sacred spaces all had spiritual directions of great significance. These were East and West, following the daily movement of the Sun. Stars, the uraeus (cobra), and lotus flowers were common sacred decorations, as was the ankh. During magickal rituals, the Four Directions were called upon as the Sons of Horus.

Magicians who used knot magick were known to the Egyptians as "blowers on knots,"[5] and could be either male or female. The binding and releasing of knots (weaving spells) while reciting incantations has long been closely connected with magick. A knot in a cord held the magick fast until the magician chose to release the spell's power.

Lamps were lit in all temples for ceremonies, and especially on the night of the New Year. Plutarch wrote that the Egyptians kept eternal flames burning before their divine images. A symbol of purity and goodness, the lamp had the power to dispel spiritual darkness and evil forces.

Certain goddesses were associated with mirrors: Hathor, Isis, Mut, and Bast. The Egyptian mirror was a flat, oval piece of polished copper with a wooden handle. These mirrors often had a cat image at the top or on the handle. Mirrors were primarily used to reflect back evil, bad luck, and dark magick.

The sistrum (sistra, plural) also honored Hathor, Bast, Isis, Nephthys, and other goddesses. This musical instrument consisted of a looped frame with three or four rods stretched across the loop; these rods were strung with little pieces of metal. On the top of the loop was an image of a cat's head; at the bottom, where the loop fitted into the handle, the face of Isis was on one side, the face of Nephthys on the other. The sistrum was held in the right hand and shaken, according to Plutarch. Egyptian magicians said that the sistrum drove away the powers of darkness and all evil spirits.[6]

A sistrum

4. Manfred Lurker, *The Gods & Symbols of Ancient Egypt.*
5. Budge, *Amulets & Superstitions.*
6. This ancient belief was later twisted by Christians and said to be the property of church bells.

The sistrum had very spiritual meanings attached to it. The curved loop symbolized the orbit of the Moon, which the Goddess (the cat image at the top) controlled. The four rods represented the four Elements, while the sound was the mingling of the Elements during magickal rites.[7]

The effectiveness of the ritual or spell was believed to be affected by the purity of the priest or magician. Therefore, purification beforehand was considered necessary. This could be a ritual bath or a simple handwashing; basins before the temple gates provided water for those who would enter. The classical writer Apuleius wrote that part of the initiation ceremonies for the Isis Mysteries included a ritual bath, during which the initiate had water poured over him or her, as in a baptism.

The ancient Egyptians believed that every word held power, particularly when employed in magick. Whether this word power was creative or destructive depended on the intent of the user.

When spellworking required writing, this was done primarily in black or red ink. Instructions follow certain chapters of the *Egyptian Book of the Dead*, which was written in hieroglyphics; these instructions, written in red ink, are called rubrics. In a few instances, however, as in the *Book of Overthrowing Apep*, the magician is told to write Apep's name in green ink.

The Egyptians taught that certain words, uttered by trained magicians, could gain the desired results. These words were also considered to be powerful if written on parchment and worn or carried by a person.

Like the Babylonians, the Egyptian magicians used divining cups or bowls. These copper or gold vessels were filled to the brim with water and gazed into while asking a question. A modern substitute could be a crystal ball or a polished slab of black onyx.[8]

Wax figures were also used by Egyptian magicians, as reported by Theocritus in the *Pharmakeutria*. These figures were modeled as closely as possible to the features and form of the person to be affected by the magick. These ceremonies could be either positive or negative. The Arab writer Abu-Shaker, who lived in the thirteenth century c.e., told of such figures that were nailed to the inside of a box; this was to prevent the people represented by the figures from harming the box's owner.

---

7. Budge, *The Gods of the Egyptians*.
8. Check with Abyss, 48 Chester Rd., Chester, MA 01011 for crystal balls and onyx mirrors or slabs.

We know from the Westcar Papyrus of the Fourth Dynasty that Egyptian magicians kept their personal materials for working magick in a special box. The magician Ubaner, mentioned in the papyrus, had a box of ebony and white gold along with an ebony rod. No description is given of this wand, but we do know that Babylonian medical magicians used rods entwined by two serpents, the forerunner of the modern medical sign, the caduceus.

Although we are most familiar with structured Egyptian magick, whose details are found in surviving ancient records, it is probable that many of these ancient magicians worked in ways similar to magicians of today—from the heart and the need and the intuition of the moment. The majority of them could not afford gold and ebony wands, gold divining cups, or ivory amulets. They made do with what they had on hand and had the same success rate as those flourishing expensive ritual tools. The power of magick never comes from ideal conditions, elaborate surroundings, expensive tools, or fancy robes. It can only come from deep within the magician. It is powered by belief and need.

I have tried to keep the following spells as simple in materials as possible. If a spell calls for something you don't have, can't find, or haven't the money to buy, substitute something else. For example, a wand can be as simple as a small twig; white candles can replace any other color; a deity name or a stamped image on paper can replace a statue. Stick, cone, or loose incense are interchangeable; if you find you've run out of incense, use perfume or shaving cologne. If fresh flowers are out of season or unavailable, substitute artificial ones; even wild flowers or a bouquet of wild grasses will do.

A good magician doesn't worry about not having expensive materials but rather with successfully completing a spellworking. A true magician also knows that knowledge comes from doing, and will never hold back because she or he might not know everything.

If you are already into magickal activities, the following spells can be incorporated into a ritual, complete with cast circle and calling of quarters. However, it is not vital or necessary to do so. These spells are complete on their own.

Note: Light of the Moon refers to the time just after the New Moon and including the Full Moon. Dark of the Moon refers to the time just after the Full Moon and including the New Moon.

Mollie: The Witch's Cat

I have a cat. Her eyes are green.
She's fat and very, very black.
She cries and talks with all her might,
And sleeps with me on moonless nights.

But when the moon is full and bright,
She takes a sudden fancy flight.
She sits aback me on my broom.
Our shadows cut across the moon.

We fly around, the world below,
Our good and warding spells bestow.
And after all our deeds are done,
We creep into bed before the Sun does rise.

We arise when the misty eve draws nigh,
Before the moon is set in the sky.
The witches' cauldron bubbles and steams
And Mollie and I drink the brew of spells and dreams.

—JOYCE SMITH

Cat Spells[9]

Human Healing

Materials: Statue of Bast[10] and/or Sekhmet or of a black cat. Picture of the human to be healed, or at least their name written on a piece of paper. Green thread. A white or blue candle. Incense: lavender, lotus, or myrrh.[11]

Timing: Healing should be done any time that it is needed; repeat the spellworking on the next Full Moon to reinforce and strengthen the healing power.

Other Advice: Be certain that the person in question really wants a healing, otherwise you will be fighting against their desire. It is better to ask that person, if possible. If they are not open to Pagan ways, you can use the term "pray for you." Oftentimes both the magician and the patient must learn when to let go and let life end in its natural course.

Spell

Set up a little altar or sacred space, arranging the statues to the rear of your working area. Place the candle to the side of the statue or in between if you are using two statues. Light the candle and the incense.

Place the picture or paper with the name of the person needing to be healed on the altar directly in front of you. In your own words, and using the sick person's name, ask the Goddess to be kind and grant healing. Sit quietly for a time, visualizing a stream of healing blue light coming from the candle and blending into the picture or paper before you.

---

9. All of these spells can be done without any further ritual training. However, for those involved in full rituals and the casting of circles, these can be performed in this manner also.

10. An excellent place to buy inexpensive and beautiful statues of Bast or almost any other goddess or god is from JBL Statues, P.O. Box 163, Rt. 1, Box 246, Crozet, VA 22932; their excellent catalog only costs $3.00 and is well worth the money. JBL has statues of such feline deities as Bast, Sekhmet, Freyja, and others. Rubber stamps of cats (which can be used to create pictures to take the place of statues) can be purchased from Stamp Magic, P.O. Box 60874, Longmeadow, MA 01116; their catalog is $2.00 and has stamps for all kinds of cats, including the big wild ones.

11. For more excellent information on incenses and oils, read *The Complete Book of Incense, Oils & Brews* by Scott Cunningham, published by Llewellyn.

When the blue light ceases, take the green thread and cut off a piece thirteen inches long. If you are using a paper with a name written on it, roll the paper into a small cylinder and wrap the green thread around it several times, tying it when you are finished. If you are working with a photo, just loosely wrap the thread about the photo. Do the thread wrapping while chanting:

> *Renewing green, healing blue,*
> *I bind these energies into you.*
> *As threads about your image wind,*
> *Perfect healing to you I bind.*

Lay the thread-wrapped photo or paper near the statue, leaving it there until the candle is burned out. Burn the thread and paper (if you are using a photo, remove the thread to be burned and return the photo to the proper person), and dispose of the ashes and candle wax.

 ## Cat (Animal) Healing

Materials: Statue of Bast and/or Sekhmet or of a black cat. Picture of the cat (or animal) to be healed, or at least their name written on a piece of paper. Green thread. A blue or white candle. Incense: lavender, lotus, or myrrh.

Timing: Healing should be done any time that it is needed; repeat the spellworking on the next Full Moon to reinforce and strengthen the healing power.

Other Advice: Be certain that the animal in question really wants a healing, otherwise you will be fighting against their intuitive instincts. Cats and other animals usually have more spiritual sense than humans when it comes to knowing when it is time to leave life. Oftentimes the magician must learn when to let go and let life end in its natural course.

Spell

Set up a little altar or sacred space, arranging the statues to the rear of your working area. Place the candle to the side of the statue or in between if you are using two statues. Light the candle and the incense.

With the photo or paper with the sick animal's name on it before you, ask the goddess Bast to grant healing. Take as much time as you feel you need to express this petition.

Sit quietly for a time, visualizing a stream of healing blue light coming from the candle and blending into the picture or paper before you.

When the blue light ceases, take the green thread and cut off a piece thirteen inches long. If you are using a paper with a name written on it, roll the paper into a small cylinder and wrap the green thread around it several times, tying it when you are finished. If you are working with a photo, just loosely wrap the thread about the photo. Do the thread wrapping while chanting:

> *Lady of cats, large and small,*
> *Answer my entreating call.*
> *Cast out the sickness, bring the Light.*
> *Grant loving healing through Thy might.*
> *Renewing green, healing blue,*
> *I bind these energies into you.*
> *As threads about your image wind,*
> *Perfect healing to you I bind.*

Lay the thread-wrapped photo or paper near the statue, leaving it there until the candle is burned out. Burn the thread and paper (if you are using a photo, remove the thread to be burned and return the photo to the proper person) and dispose of the ashes and candle wax.

A statue of Bast

Finding a True Love

Materials: Castoff fur from a female cat. A small vase of flowers. A
red or pink candle. Incense: rose, musk, or jasmine. A small red
or pink cloth bag. A red heart cut from paper or a heart charm. Dried
rose petals in a small dish.

Timing: Light of the Moon or the Full Moon.

Other Advice: Under no circumstances should this or any love spell
be used to influence a particular person. Humans have a bad habit of
getting a fixation on someone who either doesn't love them in return or
who isn't right for them. By attempting to influence a particular person,
you can create a lot of heartache and karma for yourself.

Spell

Set up a little altar or sacred space, arranging the candle in the center at the rear
of your working area. Place the flowers a safe distance from the candle and out
of your immediate way. Put the dish with the rose petals directly in front of you.
Light the candle and the incense.

Spend some time seriously thinking about the qualities you desire in a true
love. Don't stop at just physical appearance, but decide what you would like in
character and morals. Take the cat fur into your power hand (usually the hand
with which you write). Breathe gently onto the fur and place it in the dish with
the rose petals.

Hold your hand over the dish and chant:

> *Use all your powers of wisdom and persuasion,*
> *All you cats in the astral worlds.*
> *Guide me to my perfect true love*
> *That we may have a joyful life. Thank you.*

Carefully put the rose petals, the red paper heart (or charm), and the cat fur
into the small bag. If you desire, you can add three drops of rose oil to the bag,
also. Either carry the bag with you or keep it in a safe place in your home. When
you feel the spell has achieved its end, return the petals and fur back to Nature;
burn the paper heart. The heart charm can be worn on a necklace or added to
your key ring.

If you want to intensify the spell, repeat it three, five, or seven times. When repeating this spell, instead of restuffing the bag, simply hold the closed bag in your hands while chanting.

Attracting Prosperity

Materials: Castoff whiskers. A small green or brown cloth bag. Mint oil and dried mint leaves. A piece of paper and a pencil. A green or brown candle. Incense: cinnamon, bergamot, ginger, or pine.

Timing: Light of the Moon or Full Moon.

Other Advice: Don't expect opportunities or riches to fall into your lap after doing prosperity spells. Instead, you need to become aware of everything that happens around you. Opportunities, large and small, will come your way, but it is up to you to do the work.

Spell

Set up a little altar or sacred space, arranging the candle in the center at the rear of your working area. Place the whiskers and mint leaves in a small dish, with the bag beside it. Light the candle and incense.

Write on the paper the things you would do if you were granted prosperity. Be truthful. If you really don't plan to give to charity, for example, don't say you will.

Fold the paper into a small square and put it into the bag. Add the whiskers and mint leaves, then add three drops of mint oil.

Hold the bag in both hands and say:

> *As your whiskers guide you in darkness,*
> *Guide me to my prosperity.*
> *As your whiskers warn you of possible danger,*
> *Warn me when I step aside from this path I seek.*
> *Prosperity in all things, I ask.*
> *Cat energy, bring me opportunities.*

Carry the bag with you or leave it in a safe place at home. If you wish, you can place a drop of mint oil in your billfold or purse to help draw prosperity.

Seeking Protection

Materials: Enough child's clay to make a small figure. A small cardboard or wooden box. A small, thin nail. Castoff claws. Incense: patchouli, bay, frankincense, or pine. Two small pieces of paper and a pencil. A metal bowl or cauldron. Statue or picture of Sekhmet. Sistrum or bell.

Timing: Dark of the Moon or New Moon. If it is necessary to do this spell during the light of the Moon, repeat it at the New Moon to reinforce and strengthen it.

Other Advice: You have every right to protect yourself, your family, pets, and belongings from malicious and hateful people. However, you don't have the right to demand a horrendous punishment, regardless of how you feel. Even with rapists, murderers, spouse abusers, and child molesters you should take care to state that "they be caught by their own actions and words and punished to the full extent of the law." Keep your own emotions out of it or you might find yourself involved more than you like.

Spell

Set up a little altar or sacred space, arranging the statue of Sekhmet in the center at the rear of your working area. Light the incense.

With a small amount of the clay, make a rough human form. You don't have to be an artist; just make sure it has two arms, two legs, a head, and body. Stick the castoff claws into the body of the image.

If you are being harassed by a particular person, you can write that person's name on both pieces of paper. However, it is safer to write a statement such as "all those who wish me and mine ill." Other statements could be: "the one who preys on (person's or animal's name)"; "all those who prey on and harm women (children, animals)"; "the murderer (rapist, abuser) of (person's or animal's name)."

Place one of the papers on top of the clay image and push the nail through the paper into the figure. Put the figure into the small box.

Ring the bell or sistrum three times over the figure while saying:

Avenging Sekhmet, bind this (these) evil doer(s)
In shackles which cannot be broken.
Let his (her) own body be poisoned with his (her) negativity.
Let him (her) be impotent in harming others.
Make his (her) thoughts unclear, his (her) life chaos,
His (her) mouth condemning of him (her)self.
Let Your great power protect me and mine.

Take the second paper, light it, and drop it in the metal bowl or cauldron to burn to ashes. Ring the sistrum or bell three times and say:

The attacker tastes his (her) just rewards.
Their life is bitter; mine is sweet.
No evildoer can escape the wrath of Sekhmet.

When the paper ashes are cool, put them in the box with the clay figure. Bury the box in the Earth while saying:

By the power of Sekhmet and the Earth,
You are bound forever. So mote it be.

Sekhmet

Building Courage

Materials: Statue or picture of a big wild cat (tigers or leopards are best) and/or of Sekhmet. A charm or piece of jewelry of a feline. Incense: clove or carnation.

Timing: Anytime it is needed, but best done during the light of the Moon.

Other Advice: Most of the time we need courage to face small challenges, not huge life-threatening ones. These challenges can be facing an ex-lover or ex-spouse who always knows how to push our buttons; a spouse or lover who is overstepping the bounds in some way; a boss; the nosy, bossy relative or "friend"; or even when facing a new job or class.

Spell

Set up a little altar or sacred space, arranging the picture or statue at the rear of your working area. Light the incense.

Take the feline jewelry or charm in your power hand (usually the hand with which you write) and look at the statue or picture. Imagine yourself facing the person or coming event that is giving you problems. See Sekhmet and a huge tiger or leopard standing by your side, guiding and protecting you.

Slowly pass the jewelry through the incense smoke while saying:

I stand in the shadow of Sekhmet.

I am a tiger, fearless in my power.

I am a leopard, cunning and bold.

I have courage that no one can take from me.

I am confident and secure in myself.

Wear the jewelry when facing your adversaries, and remember to smile and remain calm. Adversaries hate people who smile and are unaffected by their malicious attitude.

Desiring a Child

Materials: Castoff fur from a female cat. Statue or picture of a kitten. A charm or piece of jewelry of a kitten or cat with kittens. Pink, blue, and white candles. Incense: lotus, gardenia, or sandalwood.

Timing: Light of the Moon or the Full Moon.

Other Advice: When spelling for a child, take care that you aren't hoping the child will mend a rocky relationship or marriage, or get someone to marry you; this never works. Also take care that you aren't obsessed with "owning" a child who will take care of you in your old age. No one "owns" another person, nor should anyone be under an obligation of that kind. Parents are merely temporary caretakers and teachers of their children. It is a grueling, high-stress position that lasts for at least eighteen years. Think about it carefully.

Spell

Set up a little altar or sacred space, arranging the candles at the rear of your working area with the white candle in the center, the blue candle on your left, and the pink on your right. Light the incense and the white candle. Place the castoff fur in front of you with the charm or jewelry on top of it.

Light the blue candle and say:

Child of promise, child of love,
My spiritual longing calls to you.

Light the pink candle and say:

Child of my heart, come to me.
Bless my life with your presence.

Take the fur and jewelry and pass them slowly through the incense smoke seven times. Wear the jewelry and put the fur into a safe place (a little bag or small dish); each night when you take off the jewelry, place it back on the fur.

Facing Birth

Materials: Castoff fur from a female cat (if for a human) or castoff fur from the female cat facing birth. A small cloth bag. Statue or picture of kittens; also one of Bast. Incense: jasmine or wisteria.

Timing: Whenever necessary, but preferably before birth pains start. If you have a reliable Pagan friend, he or she can repeat this spell while you are in labor. If you are doing this for an animal, do the spell before the labor begins; then spend time comforting the mother during the labor.

Other Advice: There is little way to know beforehand if a birth (human or animal) will have complications, so be certain that you see a physician and your pet sees a veterinarian regularly before the birth time.

Spell

Set up a little altar or sacred space in a place where it can be left until the birth is completed. Arrange the statue and picture in the center at the rear of this space. Light the incense and say:

> *Gentle Bast, hold me (person's or animal's name) in Your loving hands.*
> *Let the birth of the coming child (children) be easy.*
> *Keep all fear and negativity far from me (her).*
> *Be at my (her) side as the child (children) enter(s) this world.*
> *I place my trust in you, Bast.*

Gently brush the castoff fur against your cheeks, thinking of Bast's love and goodness. Put the fur into the bag and leave it by the statue on the altar. Leave it there until the birth is over.

Whenever you feel fear or dread of the coming birth, open the little bag and breathe your fears gently into it. If you are fearful for your cat, perform the same gesture.

Spiritual Growth

Materials: Castoff whiskers; statues or pictures of Bast and Isis. A stamp or picture of a cat's paw print. Incense: lotus, jasmine, or frankincense. A cat's eye stone (this can be set in jewelry if you want to wear it afterwards). Two white candles.

Timing: Light of the Moon or Full Moon if you are trying to understand Upperworld powers; dark of the Moon or New Moon if you are struggling to understand the mysterious Underworld powers.

Other Advice: Spiritual growth isn't a one-time "I've got it" proposition. Ideally, it is a continuous, upward spiral of knowledge-seeking that never ends. Sometimes a metaphorical light will come on, and we will understand a single spiritual point with great clarity. Most of the time, however, we have to plod along, step by step, sweating for everything we learn. What we learn through patience and perseverance usually lasts the longest.

Spell

Set up a little altar or sacred space, arranging one candle on each side at the rear of your working area. Place the statues of Bast and Isis between the candles. Set the picture of the cat's paw print at the foot of the statues, with the cat's eye stone and the whiskers on top of it.

Light the incense. Lay your hands over the paw print, whiskers, and stone, saying:

> *I seek guidance on my spiritual path.*
> *I am led to the Truth by the track of the cat.*
> *By the eye of the cat I see through spiritual darkness into the Light where all things are made clear.*
> *By the whiskers of the cat, I am guided in the right way.*
> *The Ladies of Wisdom speak to my heart and soul.*
> *Their words enter my dreams, guiding and instructing me.*
> *I seek Truth and Light!*

Sit quietly for a few moments while you think over the spiritual ideas you want clarified or the difficulties you have in deciding upon a spiritual path to take. When you are finished, put out the candles. The candles, whiskers, and paw print can be reused whenever you wish to repeat this spell.

The cat's eye stone can be carried or worn in jewelry as a reminder that you are being guided with wisdom and clarity.

Answers often come in unexpected ways: dreams, talking with others, reading a book, et cetera. Be open and aware.

Saying Farewell

Materials: Picture of the human or cat (or other animal) who has died. Statues or pictures of Bast and Isis. A goblet of fresh water and a small amount of salt. Incense: frankincense. A white and a black candle.

Timing: Whenever it is needed and the time best for those participating.

Other Advice: Called a wake by the Irish, the farewell for someone who has died is a very important method of facing reality and releasing emotions, which if not released properly can cause great problems. No one, male or female, should try for the stiff upper lip—it isn't mentally healthy. Have plenty of tissue on hand, and give anyone who needs it the luxury of letting it all out.

Spell

Set up a little altar or sacred space, arranging the black candle on the left and the white candle on the right at the rear of your working area. Place the statues between the candles with the picture of the deceased in front of them. The goblet of water and dish of salt can be set to one side.

Light both candles and say:

> *We are gathered here to remember (person's or animal's name). Our sorrow is great because we can no longer touch and hold him (her), for we are still bound by a physical body while he (she) is free in an ethereal form.*

Drop a pinch of salt into the goblet and gently swirl it to mix. Say:

> *Salt and water, symbols of eternal creation.*
> *The taste of water and salt reminds us of the blood which keeps our physical*
>   *bodies alive,*
> *Yet it also reminds us of the sea, the water of the womb, and the sacredness*
>   *of the eternal circle of all life.*
> *(Name), we release you to the rest you need, knowing that one day,*
>   *in another time and place, once more we shall meet and know and*
>   *love again.*

Lightly sprinkle drops of the salted water over the altar. Put out the black candle, saying:

> *You have cast off the Earthly body by which we knew you,*

Put out the white candle and say:

> *But you have put on another body, one of joy and Light.*
> *Remember us.*

Now is the time for everyone present to recall pleasant, happy, and funny remembrances of the deceased. If there are tears, recognize them as part of the healing process.

2

Cat Tales

Cats have always been considered clairvoyant, capable of seeing ghosts, able to communicate by telepathy, and to predict earthquakes, storms, volcanic eruptions, and other disasters. The most interesting cat tales come from personal experiences of cat lovers and owners. Not all of the following stories are of psychic happenings; one is a delightful fantasy tale of the first order.

> I love cats because I enjoy my home;
> and little by little, they become its visible soul.
>
> —JEAN COCTEAU

Flash

When we lost our cat Samuel Tibbs to fatal urinary tract infections, I made it plain I didn't want any more cats for a while. "But, Mom," my daughter Sharon said, "we have to save the kitten at the truck farm. They've let the dogs kill all but this one!" So we ended up with a tiny little striped male who was christened Flash, because he ran fast enough to stay alive.

25

Flash had such a laid-back personality that few people realized, until too late, that he also was a calculated and deliberate prankster. If he was teased, he could wait for days to get his revenge, which usually took the form of attack in dark rooms or dragging socks all over the floor. He would deliberately ambush Buckwheat (the dog), when least expected, by swatting his nose from concealment in the herb bed. He loved to lie on the porch roof and stare down at visitors, or children at Halloween, until they got nervous.

Flash was also extremely psychic. Just before Mt. St. Helens erupted in May of 1980, he began to be very nervous. He wanted close but would bite if anyone touched him. This was unusual behavior for Flash, and took everyone by surprise. He lost weight during the eruption and aftershocks, and was always close to someone. After that, we noticed that he reacted to any eruption or earthquake around the Pacific Ocean. He gave about two weeks' notice of such events by his behavior.

We learned to watch his behavior also in regard to the character of people. Flash would instantly know whether someone was untrustworthy, potentially dangerous, or just a nuisance. Nuisances he dealt with by getting in their lap at every opportunity and working his claws right through the skin of their legs. Those who were untrustworthy he glared at, then turned and walked away with his nose in the air. With potentially dangerous people he left the house and wouldn't return until they left.

To him, magick circles, meditations, and trances were old hat, something he had obviously been part of through many lifetimes. He could be off mouse hunting on the farthest edge of the property when any of these things began. However, it would only be a matter of a few minutes before he appeared and demanded to take part. He never missed a single occasion.

He died of a brain tumor shortly before we moved to another town. Although we took his ashes with us and buried them on the new property, I wondered if Flash would come along in spirit. He didn't let us down. During the first circle we held, there he was: a shadowy figure near the altar, intently watching every move. "Of course I'm here," he seemed to say, a smug smile on his face. "Somebody has to keep all the spirits in line."

—D. J. CONWAY

Welcome to the Cat Blues Cafe

I was waiting for our management meeting to start when one of the other managers happened to comment on a garnet ring I was wearing. "My cats bought this for me for my birthday," I told him. Our company president heard my comment and asked, "How did they pay for it?" "Well, with Stanley's MasterCat card," I quipped, expecting everyone to laugh. The room became very quiet and I squirmed with embarrassment as I realized they were all waiting for an explanation.

"Stanley is a big black enterprising cat who was bored with the traditional occupation of mousing, fighting with the neighbor cats, and caring for his human. One day, quite out of the blue, he asked me if he could start a couple of catnip patches around our yard. I asked him what he planned to do with so much catnip and he said he had an idea for making money. Later that same day, he asked if he could borrow my car as he walked out the door with the keys in tow. I watched out the window as he adjusted his red beret and put on his black horned-rimmed sunglasses with one lens missing. He backed the car out of the driveway and was gone in a flash. I didn't worry as Stanley had a perfect driving record and he always replaced the gas he used in his jaunts.

"When he returned, he was very excited. He called his Siamese brothers, Ziggy and Barney, into a meeting under my bed. They were there for what seemed like an eternity. Finally, they emerged and announced they were going into business together. Stanley said if I would plant the catnip, they would tend it and harvest it in the fall. In return for my support, I would be 'treated very well.'

"All summer long, the three boys would disappear most afternoons and evenings. The catnip grew and spread. That fall we harvested the catnip and Stanley placed it in a huge white basket to dry. All winter long, Stanley wrapped catnip cigarettes and packed them in boxes. I was dying to ask about their plans, but I figured they would tell me when it was time for me to know. Actually, it was fun to speculate about what they might be up to.

"As the winter snow melted, there was heightened energy in our house. I noticed my telephone bills were quite high, but the boys assured me they would take care of all the extra expenses. As spring grew into summer, our cat family seemed perfectly happy and normal, for the most part.

"One very sultry August night, I just couldn't fall asleep. I don't know if it was the heat or the full moon. I got out of bed and went outside for some air. The yard was lit by the moon and I could see all around me that shadow side of life. Leaning up against a utility pole in our back yard, gazing at the moon, I contemplated the wonder of it all in an almost dreamlike state of mind. Suddenly, I was startled by movement in the high grass behind our row of pine trees. My heart was pounding as I took shelter in the neighbor's trees behind me. A beautiful white Persian cat, dressed in a scarlet beaded gown, emerged from under our pines. She was escorted by a fine looking Siamese dressed in a brown suit, fedora and spats. My Barney! They strolled down the corridor between the pines and our wild flower garden, disappearing into the night.

"I held my breath as I watched cat after cat arrive and leave the pine grove. All dressed in finery, all walking on their hind legs and talking as you and I would talk on a night on the town. Finally, around 1 A.M., I could stand there no longer. I walked up to what seemed to be the entrance and peered under the bows. I saw only darkness, but I could hear MUSIC and laughter! Glasses were clinking and the air was smokey. Had my imagination finally run away with me? Was this really happening? Was it a dream? A rustling in the grass near me caused me to leap in the air and run as fast as I could back into the house and into my bed.

"The next morning, as I fed Stanley, Ziggy, and Barney, all seemed normal. Finally, I could wait no more and said, 'I think I know what you boys have been up to and I want a complete explanation.' Stanley sauntered over to a throw rug and washed his face. He then told me of his new business, the Cat Blues Cafe. The boys had hired union groundhogs to dig a huge underground facility, with its opening under the pine trees. Cool cats from miles around could come and enjoy the finest blues, the sweetest cream, the smelliest fish, the strongest catnip and each other's good company. And come they did, every Friday and Saturday night.

"The years passed; so did Ziggy and Barney. Stanley was alone trying to run the Cat Blues Cafe from the first warm weekend in April until the last warm weekend in October. One May, two lovely Oriental Shorthairs, Morgan Le Fay, a lynx colorpoint, and Nimue, a silver-ticked tabby, came to live with us. Long and lean, with deep Siamese-like voices, it didn't take Stanley long to recognize talent. He offered them jobs as waitresses and 'entertainers' at the Cat Blues Cafe. He dressed them in sequined gowns, broad-brimmed hats with long, soft feathers and fine white elbow-length gloves. Morgan's dress was periwinkle blue, to match her eyes. Nimue's gown was deep emerald green, which brought out both the green of her eyes and also the silver shimmer of her fur. Breathtaking beauties!

"Stanley told me of Morgan's talent to get up before the crowd, with a flute of cream in one paw and a long cigarette holder smoldering with catnip smoke in the other, and belt out the blues for hours at a time. Nimue's talent was in teasing the young male cats with her feathers and cajoling them into spending their money on food, drink and gambling. Stanley had his special chair in the back of the room, where he could keep an eye (the one golden orb not hidden by the lens of his sunglasses) on things. His red beret cocked to the side, a catnip jay hanging from his lips and his hind feet up on the chair in front of him, he watched the fruit of his labors and the enjoyment he brought to so many cats.

"Last season Stanley retired for health reasons and handed over the business to Morgan and Nimue, who have spent the winter sewing new gowns, ordering new hats, arranging gigs for various bands and making plans for some improvements, including expansion to include a large carpeted floor. I asked if this was to be a dance floor and got some very curious looks from the two of them. 'Cats don't dance, you silly thing,' they replied in unison. They told me the carpet would be covered in loose catnip and it would be used for, well, rolling. Of course, without the rock. I should have known."

I looked around the room and all of the managers' eyes were glassy, as if in a daze. I looked at the clock and realized I had monopolized much of our meeting time. The president cleared his throat and I thought, I am in some serious trouble. "Now, when are you going to write the story?" he asked with a sly smile. Someday.

—SHADOWCAT

Rezel

I lived with my cat, Rezel, in a second-floor apartment, which was located in a rambling, brick Victorian structure. Rezel was strictly an indoor cat and not very adventuresome, but one evening when I returned home from work, she insisted upon going outside. I followed her as she trundled down the staircase. She hurried over to the door that led to the building's basement, stood up on her hind feet, and frantically tapped the doorknob with her right front paw.

I had always spoken to Rezel in human talk, as most cat owners do, so I asked her, "Rezel, is there something down in the basement?" Rezel meowed, tapped the doorknob again, and looked back at me pleadingly over her shoulder.

I immediately envisioned a cat trapped in the basement and asked, "Is there a kitty in the basement?" Upon hearing the word "kitty," Rezel proceeded to meow eloquently, lashing her tail to and fro.

I opened the door, admittedly feeling a little foolish for listening to my cat. Rezel retreated quietly under the staircase and watched the door. I called out, "Here, kitty, come out, kitty," and also stood back next to Rezel. I didn't expect anything to materialize but I was wrong.

Within a few minutes, a large, male Siamese cat emerged through the doorway. He went over to Rezel, touched her nose with his, then looked up at me, flipped his tail, and stalked off toward his home. He obviously was giving credit to whom it was due for his rescue.

There are two aspects of this event that I find inexplicable. First, that Rezel was able to effectively communicate the existence of a problem and its solution. Second was her knowledge that the problem existed. From her observation area in the apartment, there was no way she could have seen whether the basement door was open or closed, nor could she have heard a cat meowing in the brick basement. I can only conclude that the trapped cat sent psychic distress signals and Rezel, who had always shown sensitivity toward suffering creatures, picked them up. She, in turn, had to communicate psychically with me so the problem could be solved. Rezel never showed an inclination to visit the basement again and was disinterested in going outside afterward as well.

—JEAN FRITZ

Cats Who Love Magick

My two current feline companions, Nimue (black, longhaired female) and Gwydion (black, shorthaired male), insist on being present when I do spellwork and complain loudly if I attempt to exclude them. If I close a door between us, they will yowl, scratch at the door, and even hurl themselves against it. They seem to know when magick is afoot, for they don't act this way at other times. However, on the rare times when I've worked with other practitioners, neither

cat has chosen to participate.

I often work using as an altar a round, clear glass coffee table, with the legs aligned to the four directions. The cats station themselves under the table, where they almost always remain, quietly attentive, from the moment I cast the circle to the time I open it. They also seem able to move in and out of the circle, as they occasionally do, to no ill effect.[1]

It is very evident that both Gwydion and Nimue can sense magical energy, are strongly attracted to it, and like bonding with me on this plane. I believe there may also be a desire on their part to guard the circle and contribute their energy to the work at hand. Although I'm aware of their energy, it feels comfortable and never distracting.

I've lived with many other cats over the years, none of whom showed much interest in magick.

—CERRIDWEN

Fascino

My present cat Osiris is and isn't my second cat. I believe he is the reincarnation of the Fascino I knew in my early twenties. I named the first kitten, who was half Persian, half Siamese, Fascino because he was fascinated with everything. During the eighteen years he lived with me, he never clawed drapes or furniture, used his claws during play, or cared for the usual cat toys or catnip. We were very close, and he was definitely "my" cat. He died of renal failure four years ago.

As I was coming home from work late one night a year and a half ago, I nearly ran over a small gray kitten in the road. I knew it was probably from a litter produced by a wild barn cat but went back to it anyway. As soon as I called, the kitten came running to me, an unusual reaction for a feral cat. I took him home and cleaned him up. Because he has the double-triangle of Isis and Osiris running from the upper point between his ears to the lower point at the center of his throat, I named him Osiris. As I understand it, this symbol has to do with life and death and rebirth, which made an extraordinary amount of sense when I began to see uncanny similarities with Fascino.

Osiris has the same huge green-brown eyes with blue centers that Fascino had. Like Fascino, he has never used his claws, stays on chairs rather than tables or countertops, and prefers to play with paper bags and knotted knee hose. He doesn't like catnip and has been "my" cat from the first day. There is no doubt that Osiris is the same cat as Fascino, right down to the sound of his voice, his mannerisms, and the way he relates to everything around him. He also answers to Fascino as well as to Osiris. I have no doubts that Fascino is back.

—S. SHELTON

---

1. *Author's note:* It is a fact that most cats can move into and out of a magick circle without disturbing the flow of energy. They are also some of the very best healers and co-magicians I have ever known.

Sabbath

For seventeen years my life included a longhaired black furball officially known as Sabbath (informally dubbed with a variety of monikers). My mother called him FatCat. My French grandmother dubbed him "Sabbath," with the accent on the second syllable. What my boyfriend called him was unprintable; to me he was my Dabby Doo.

Last June the formidable FatCat refused to eat—an unprecedented phenomenon. He was weak and couldn't be coaxed from his favorite spot, my pillow. I had gotten used to sleeping with a cat on my head and fur up my nose on a regular basis. Sabbath was uncharacteristically listless, so I rushed him to the only emergency veterinarian I could find.

For the next three days, I drove forty miles on my lunch hour to visit him until the results of the test were in. The diagnosis was liver failure, and I had to make the most heart-rending decision of my life. That evening I held him in my arms while the vet administered the shot that would end his suffering and his life. Both the vet and I were crying at the end. I took the next day off work and agonized over whether I had done the right thing for the right reasons. I cried myself to sleep every night for over a week until something unexpected happened.

I went to bed as usual, turning off the light and rolling onto my side to go to sleep, when I heard this monstrously loud purring all around my head. I assumed it was my other feline friend, but then I heard the dry food in the cat bowl being crunched. Just as I realized it couldn't possibly be her, I recognized Sabbath's purr. I rolled onto my back, and the purring got even louder. I lay there listening, with tears running down my cheeks. It continued for five minutes or more. When the purring finally stopped, I knew my Dabby Doo, my Sabbath, had come to let me know it was all right, that he didn't want me to worry anymore, and that he was happy.

It used to drive me crazy when he slept on my head, but I'd give just about anything right now to have to share my pillow and pass the night with fur up my nose.

—Kimberly Gibbs

The Surprise Cat

One night, while I was sleeping, I had a dream about a big gray cat who came up to my sliding glass door, and me letting him in. I woke up and didn't think too much about it. A couple of weeks later I was sitting on my couch and a cat came up to my sliding glass door, looking very surprised. It was the same cat in my dream. When I let him in, he acted like he had been in the apartment before. He stayed for a couple of days, then left. I haven't seen him since.

—TRACY CORPE

Mouse

My cat Mouse and I are spiritually very close, are constantly near one another, and share a unique rapport that has made me consider him my Familiar. He is a truly magickal creature who seems to have something about him that is otherworldly. He is basically an outdoor cat and invariably asks to be let out at some late hour, like 1 A.M. Although I'm usually up late, on the evening in question I wanted to get to sleep an hour earlier and didn't feel comfortable about letting him stay out all night, especially since the weather was apt to become cold.

I stood on the porch calling Mouse for ten minutes with no success. Mouse usually responds to my calls almost immediately. I spent another ten minutes inside, looking out the window, growing more worried and annoyed by the minute. Finally, I went to my bedroom. I pictured him in my mind and sent a message along a beam of light that should seek him out and deliver my words: "Mouse! I want to go to sleep. Come home NOW!" I sent a sense of urgency along just in case plain words failed to transmit mentally.

Within a couple of minutes I got a reply. It came in the form of Mouse's familiar voice in my head. There was no mistaking it. The clarity and volume of the *Mrrrow* was such that he could have been sitting on my shoulder making the sound in one ear. I went back to the window and within a couple of minutes Mouse came swaggering up to the door to be let in.

There have been other occasions when this psychic communication has taken place and feelings, like messages themselves, have been exchanged between us. I have noticed that, when calling Mouse mentally to return home, he responds more quickly to "I miss you, come home" than to a firm "Get your fuzzy behind home NOW!"

—ROBYN L. BROWN

A Circle of Cats

When I first moved onto the eleven oak-studded, hilly acres on the outskirts of a small town in the Central Coast region of California, there was only one cat, Smokey, who has since returned to Bast. Although I wasn't his human, he kept company with me through my solitary Esbat and Sabbat Circles, standing to the right of the censer, gazing into the smoke with slitted yellow-green eyes. His passing left a hole in my heart and rituals.

Because I missed his friendship so much, I began to look for another companion to join me in Circle. Since I felt another smokey-gray cat could be too painful, I asked my "helpers" to send a Siamese, a breed I have always been drawn to. Once I realized I was asking for what I wanted, rather than what I needed, I changed my wish to "Send the helper/s most perfect for my Work and Path." Soon afterward, Boots arrived, very pregnant, with her two sisters, Squirrel and Targette, and her mate Target. Squirrel and Targette joined my Circle that night, one to the North, the other to the West.

When the kittens were born, Max, a rather masculine gray tabby female, joined the Circle soon after her eyes opened. She'd drag her wobbling infant body into the sacred area under the old oak and sit slightly to the South of her Aunt Targette. Afterward, Boots, who waited impatiently outside the Circle, would pick her up by the neck and carry her back to the nest. So I had my companions, but somehow the space Smokey left was still echoingly empty. Something was still missing.

Last spring, while sitting on the front porch with my neighbor (Smokey's "official" human), we saw a small red kitten being tended by Black Tuesday, another of our adopted feline friends. Eventually, seven other kittens joined the first along with the cat we assumed was their mother, until we discovered he was male. One by one, the kittens have joined the Circle, as have Tuesday and Mr. Mom.

I sit under the old oak tree surrounded by thirteen cats: calico Squirrel to the North; then Siamese Cara, Spook and Pookah to the East; gray and white Hooligan, gray tabby Cricket, and Black Tuesday curve around to South. Snip (Tuesday's look-alike), brown and white Mr. Mom, and Max and Targette in identical gray stripes make up the arc to West, and Booter with her black and white splashed coat sits halfway between West and North.

Now, if you've been keeping track, you know that only makes twelve cats. This is because, just to my right, beside the censer, sits Red. His tail is curled around his toes, and his yellow-green eyes slitted as he watches the scented smoke rise.

Has Bast sent Smokey back to me in the shape of Red? Possibly, or maybe Red simply follows the directions of a gray shadow that sometimes appears near the altar. Either way, both are welcome.

—CHAMELEON SILVERCAT

The Cat Who Came to Dinner

I live in a pet-free zone. However, one winter my sister brought home an alley kitten that she had found wandering on the street. He was a cute little orange and white striped scrap of fur, so she named him Scrap. Scrap lived with us for about a week before she found him a home with friends.

One night we had ham for dinner. Scrap was so excited about the food that he leapt up on the dining room table and ran off with my dad's slice of ham. He was halfway down the stairs before anyone could react. Scrap ate the whole slice, which was about the same size he was. Scrap wasn't used to food being readily available and just wanted to get that ham while the getting was good. I'm sure he enjoyed it, though he did growl to ward off any predators while he was eating. We weren't planning to eat the piece of ham after he had dragged it through the house, but poor little Scrap didn't know that.

—NAN SKOVRAN

The Cat and the Ghost

When I was growing up, we lived in a house complete with a ghost. Only a few family members ever saw the ghost, but it never caused us any real problems. However, our white cat was always aware of the ghost each time it roamed the house and decided to make friends. After all, to a cat one world of existence is much the same as another. The cat loved to play with the ghost by running up and down the hall in a game of chase at night. To my parents and us kids the cat-ghost play was normal, but not so to visitors. Once Grandma came for a visit, and Grandma didn't believe in ghosts, or so she said. One night during the visit, she got up to see what the cat was doing, running through the hall, and encountered both cat and ghost. She refused to sleep in that house again.

—DANYKA EDWARDS

Stephanie

My cat Stephanie is a fawn-point Siamese. We always had a psychic connection. I never had to call her at feeding time; she always seemed to be waiting when I placed her bowl outside. One night I had a dream about a large rat. I usually never remember a dream of this kind. When I woke up, I saw Stephanie standing in the living room. She stays outside, so I thought she had gotten inside somehow. Then her form faded away before my eyes. I went to the back door to check on her, and there she sat, proudly offering me a large rat she had caught that night. I suppose she couldn't wait to tell me of her proud catch.

—DELORES WHEELER

Wiz and the Fairy

I have a male cat named Wizard, whom I call Wiz for short. He is a feisty Abyssinian-Siamese mixture and sleeps beside me at night. During June 1996, toward sunrise, I felt him pawing my ear and purring, making an earnest attempt to wake me. I touched his nose with my thumb and he trilled. Immediately Wiz jumped onto the window ledge and all the time his eyes were on mine. I came awake. Parting the curtain, I followed his inquisitive stare. Together, we watched a lovely summer fairy pass by outside, return once, then go gently on her way. She was a true summer fairy, and all that I recall of her now is that remarkable smile she shared with Wiz and me, a combined look of pleasure, gratitude, and trust. To live in green country, such as Oklahoma offers, is oftentimes an open invitation to the spiritual encounter of other worlds and dimensions. For those not afraid, it is a wonderful experience. Thank goodness for cats and fairy folks, and their magick!

—LEE PROSSER

Fatal Eclipses

My cat, Pretty Black Girl, died in the month of May. Pretty (her nickname) was sick in the morning and in my heart I knew the end was near for her. I hadn't noticed any symptoms and she had all her shots. She was only four years old and was solid and strong. In my search for answers to the pain her death brought, I noticed that the day she died was also the day of a solar eclipse. Six months later, two November eclipses took two more of my cats, two on the same day—one at 2 A.M. and one at 11 P.M. Ann Marie was six years old, and her son Wiggins was only six months old. Neither of them had symptoms of any illness either.

In each eclipse event, the north node opposed Taurus in my eighth house. All the cats who died were born with sun in Taurus. Not only was I their surrogate mother, but their midwife for passage to the great beyond. Fortunately, this planetary transit's path has traveled through the range of influence in my chart.

—LYNDA LEE MACKEN

Jeremy

I adopted Jeremy in February 1977 when he was eight to ten weeks old. In the late spring of 1980, my husband (then my fiancé) and I moved in with his dad, who had severe cardiac disease. My father-in-law was allergic to cats, so Jeremy stayed at my parents' house, a thirty minute drive away. I worked the 3:00 to 11:00 shift and went to my parents' house several times a week. Often the trip was unplanned and I would not telephone before driving over. My mother would know I was on my way for about ten minutes before I arrived. Jeremy would become excited and run from window to window. Sure enough, ten minutes later I would arrive.

—INGRID GORDON

Misha

Cats are gracious, tender, mischievous angels. I grew up with several cats and dogs during my childhood, but one cat stands out in my mind and heart. Samuel Tibbs Finnegan Cat, V. "Sam" was one of many in a long line of Samuels, but he was decidedly different from all the rest. Sam was a black and white neutered male that had the temperament of an angel. He was my special friend. We lived out in the country and I had few friends. You would often find him stretched out—he reached from side to side on my bed. He would always be there to greet me on my long walk home from the bus stop. But his life was cut short with urinary tract blockage, a frequent malady in neutered male cats. I was devastated.

It wasn't until I was an adult and engaged to be married that Sam found me again. I didn't go looking for a cat but found him at a friend's house. He was digging for his breakfast in their garbage can. I pulled him out and looked into his eyes. There was just something special that sparkled there. He rode on my shoulder all the way home in the car and immediately settled in. He insisted on sleeping at the end of my bed that night, and so he took his spot in my life once again.

Being a friendly cat, visitors to our home never fazed him. He, believing people were entering his domain, treated them accordingly—a sniff, maybe a rub on the legs to let them know he liked them, or an indifferent nose in the air and walking away if he didn't care (a true snubbing). Except one time—an obnoxious insurance salesman (who wouldn't take "No!" from me) went through my husband and came for an appointment at the house. I was furious but said nothing to this man when he came in. Misha (Sam) did his usual sniffing, checking-out routine. He even went so far as to invitingly rub against the man's leg. The salesman reached down to pet him and promptly got bit on the hand while Misha galloped away. I had to cover my mouth to keep from laughing out loud. Now how did he know that's exactly what I wanted to do?

Misha also loved to investigate visitors' cars, especially the inside if he could find an open window. During a remodeling project, Misha crawled into one of the carpenters' trucks and was accidentally taken about ten miles away before he escaped. I searched for over two weeks, checking with the local animal shelters, putting up "Missing" posters, but no sign of him. I kept being drawn to a particular neighborhood (in a direct line with our house) but never found him. My husband was certain he was dead, but I knew he wasn't. I kept seeing a picture of him in my mind calling to me. Finally, two weeks later, I got a call from someone who had found a black and white cat. When I drove to the house it was the exact place I had been drawn to earlier!

Misha, being half Siamese, is a very talkative, expressive cat. I was quickly "trained" that if I was to be gone for more than a day, I was to inform him ahead of time. My punishment, if I didn't, was often a not-so-gentle tackle and nip on the ankle upon my return. He never did this to anyone else. When I explained to him where I was going and when I would be back, he seemed content and no punishments were issued.

We've always been in tune with each other's wants and needs. Every time I've been sick and in bed, Misha is promptly there for me. He even goes so far as to curl up next to, or on top of, whatever body part hurts. During a particularly devastating period of my life, when I was going through a divorce, I lay in bed one night when the awful finality of it hit me. Misha was curled up at the end of the bed. I began sobbing uncontrollably. Misha lifted his head and meowed, walked up and curled up on my chest, loudly purring while I continued my cathartic weeping. This lasted for ten to fifteen minutes until my sobbing subsided. Then Misha got up and went back to his spot at the foot of my bed.

Some people say that cats are cold, aloof creatures, but I know better!

—JEANNE MCLARNEY

SECTION II

The Historical Cat

3

The Cat in Ancient History and Superstition

Members of the feline family have been involved in the social, cultural, and spiritual growth of humans from the very earliest times, as shown by wall paintings in European Paleolithic caves.

It often happens that a man is more humanely related to a cat or dog than to any human being.

—HENRY DAVID THOREAU

In ancient cultures, the cat was both a solar and a lunar animal. It was said to be psychic and could predict coming disasters and affect the weather, hence the expression "raining cats and dogs." The first pictures or representations of cats, usually lions and leopards, have been discovered in sacred Paleolithic caves.

Archaeologists know these caves were sacred to the Paleolithic cultures because of the paintings themselves and because the actual ritual chambers are so difficult to reach. All of these chambers are found deep in the caves, reached only by traversing narrow ledges and crawling through very narrow openings.[1]

On a cave wall at Les Trois Freres in France, and dating back 18,000 years, is a painting of a lioness. Her form is part of a series of great, vibrant paintings once used as part of mystic, spiritual rituals. One can imagine the cat's spirit coming alive in the flickers of the shamanic fire as the worshippers met to honor the Great Goddess and Her unending cycle of birth, death, and rebirth.

Later, in the Neolithic Goddess-culture site of Catal Huyuk in present-day Turkey, leopards and lionesses are again portrayed as powerful, magickal companions of the Great Goddess. An 8,000-year-old statue from Catal Huyuk of a Mother Goddess shows Her giving birth on Her throne; on each side of the Goddess is a leopard, the tails wrapped around Her shoulders, giving their energy to the new creation issuing from between the Goddess' thighs.

At the same site, on a wall within the ruins of a great matriarchal shrine, two leopards stand face to face, their forms molded in the plaster and richly painted in red. Called the Leopard Shrine, this ancient building must have been the site of powerful and important rituals, for studies have shown that these leopards were repeatedly replastered and painted, leaving up to forty layers of pigment.

A marble statue recovered from the ruins of Mesopotamia shows an unknown goddess with a lioness head; this has been dated to 5,000 years ago. This goddess holds her tense hand-paws in readiness, a look of deep concentration on her face, as if facing a challenge with undaunted courage.

Ancient Egypt is probably the best-known site of the veneration of cats and other felines. Thousands of statues, paintings, and amulets of feline forms have been unearthed in the Nile region.

Egyptian figures of cats often showed them with a scarab engraved on the head or chest. These statues show the Egyptian cat to be slender, long-legged, and small of head. The most sacred of these cats was black.

Little amulet-figures of cats have been found in tombs, behind walls, and under the floors of temples and houses. Some of these amulets were pierced so they can be worn. They were made of gold, silver, faience, semi-precious and precious stones. These figures of cats show them in every mood and posture, from meditative to pouncing and running. One of

Setcha, an Egyptian serpent-headed leopard (from E. A. Wallis Budge's *The Gods of the Egyptians, Vol. 1*)

---

1. Time-Life, *Early Europe: Mysteries in Stone.*

these amulet-figures was a small three-inch column with a cat and kittens on the top. Cats were also used to decorate necklaces, rings, pins, musical instruments, and scepters.[2]

In its solar aspect, the cat was immortalized in a string game called the "cat's cradle." This game, which consists of two people winding a string into a series of complicated patterns, is still played around the world. Originally, this "game" was used as sympathetic magick, such as with the Eskimos, who used it at Summer Solstice to entangle the Sun and hold it back from the winter setting, and Congo tribes, who used it to persuade the Sun to rest.[3]

The cat and serpent were long considered to be enemies by the Egyptians. Since the cat symbolized the deity idea of Virgin-Mother, the goddess Isis sometimes assumed a feline form. As Aset, Isis killed the serpent Apep in the original story, not the god Ra as later related in myth.

Bast (from Budge's *The Gods of the Egyptians, Vol. 1*)

The ancient Egyptians have long been recognized as cat lovers. They were fervent in their belief that all cats were sacred (especially to several of their goddesses) and should be protected. When Caesar conquered the Nile area, a Roman soldier killed a cat. The Roman declared that this death was accidental, but the Egyptians felt otherwise. The furious crowd lynched the soldier and dragged his body through the city. The Romans threatened reprisals, but it was too late. The Egyptians rioted, finally causing the deaths of Antony and Cleopatra.

The cat played an important part in ancient Egyptian mythology. In the *Egyptian Book of the Dead*, the male cat is called *Mau*, the female *Mait*. Initiates to the Mysteries were taught that cats knew the words to vanquish the powers of darkness; if a person loved and befriended a cat, the animal would tell you those words.

---

2. Patricia Dale-Green, *Cult of the Cat.*
3. In New Guinea, this game is played to encourage the growth of yams; when the string-game is finished, the string is used to tie up the yam stalks. Many other cultures who once used this game as a ritual have forgotten its original purpose, and the string ritual has deteriorated into a children's game.

The Egyptian goddess Bast's usual form was that of a woman with a cat head.[4] In her right hand she held a sistrum and in her left an aegis with the head

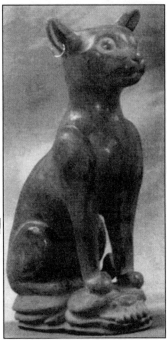

of a cat or lioness on it (an aegis, or shield, is an ancient word for a decorated sacred shield and is used by archaeologists and those trained in mythology). One ancient legend says that Bast was an incarnation of the soul of Isis. Indeed, at Dendera in Egypt, Bast was called the holy Sekhem, wife of the god An, who was a form of Osiris.[5] Shown with a cat's head, Bast represented the Moon, but when she was occasionally portrayed with the head of a lioness (usually painted green), she symbolized the sunlight.

Bubastis, the capital of the Amkent, the seventh nome of Lower Egypt, was the center of Bast, the cat goddess. Such classical writers as Herodotus, Diodorus, Strabo, and Pliny wrote of this city. Today, this site is marked by the ruins of Tell-Basta.

One statue of Bast shows her right hand holding the sistrum, symbol of lovemaking and joyous dancing, both an important part of her rituals. In her left hand she cradles a small cat figure, which is crowned with a solar disc and the sacred uraeus (cobra).

A sculptor's depiction of Bast atop a scarab

Bast's mirror-sister was the goddess Pasht (Pekheth, Pekhet, or Pekh), the cat or lioness deity of Pekhit. The name Pasht means "tearer." As Bast, this goddess kept watch at night with her Sun eyes, while as Pasht she held and pierced the head of the serpent of darkness. Near the modern village of Beni Hasan in Upper Egypt are the remains of a temple of Pasht, carved out of solid rock in the mountain.

Another Egyptian goddess often portrayed with the head of a lioness was Sekhmet. A solar goddess, Sekhmet was seen as the ruler of human fate, who usually blazed with divine fury, while Bast was gentler, the guardian of her human "litter." The opposing qualities of Bast and Sekhmet did not appear until later Egyptian times, a sign of encroaching patriarchal influence over the goddesses.

---

4. The British Museum has a huge statue of Bast. She has the forehead and ears of a cat and wears a headdress of sacred asps, each crowned by the Sun.
5. E. A. Wallis Budge, *The Gods of the Egyptians.*

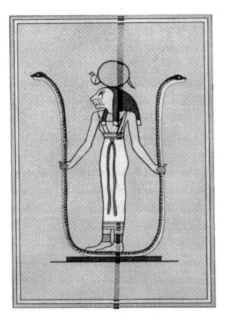

Sekhmet (from Budge's *The Gods of the Egyptians, Vol. 1*)

Not all ancient Mediterranean cultures worshipped cats, however. The Assyrians and Chaldeans were very hostile to their few wild and domestic cats. They had little, if anything, good to say about them at all. In fact, the Chaldeans would shout "Be off, accursed one," every time they saw a black cat. The Hebrews were extremely hostile to cats; only a brief phrase in Isaiah mentions them as "demons of the desert."

Ashtoreth, a Syrian goddess, was known to the Egyptians as "Mistress of Horses" and "Lady of the Chariot." They considered her to

be a form of Sekhmet–Hathor. She wore the head of a lioness and was the terrible, destructive deity of war.

In neighboring Arabia, however, they never hated cats. In fact, the Arabs have kept cats from the sixth century C.E., and from the time of Mohammed they have treated them with respect and indulgence. In fact, to the Arab peoples a dog is considered to be unclean, while a cat is to be indulged.

A legend says that Mohammed himself had a favorite cat, Muezza, who obviously slept where he pleased. One day the Prophet had to leave, but Muezza was asleep on the sleeve of his coat. Rather than disturb the cat's sleep,

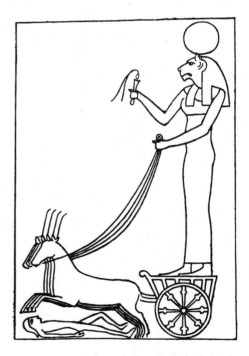

Ashtoreth (from Budge's *The Gods of the Egyptians, Vol. 2*)

Mohammed cut off the sleeve and went on about his business. When he returned, Muezza bowed his thanks. In recognition of his love for the cat, Mohammed stroked the length of Muezza's back three times. Ever since, cats have had the ability to fall on their feet.

The Persian religion of Zoroastrianism, like the Christians, divided animals into those who served good (*Ormuzd* or *Ahura Mazdah*) and those served the

A lion architectural ornament
from Ancient Greece

devil (*Ahriman*). To them, the cat was associated with Ahriman, hell, darkness, lust, and laziness.

The palace of Knossos, on the island of Crete, has a painting made of faience wall tiles. This mural dates from about 1600 B.C.E. and shows hunting cats with wild sheep. The hunting cats in this mural are very similar to those seen in Egyptian murals, possibly suggesting that one civilization learned from the other how to train cats for hunting.

According to the Greek Herodotus, in his *History*, it was Greek sailors who imported Egyptian cats; actually the first evidence of cats appears in Greece about 500 B.C.E. However, this claim isn't too plausible since the Phoenicians were sharper traders and better sailors who had trade with Egypt going before the Greeks thought of it and had an established culture long before the Greek states were in existence. The Phoenicians also ranged much farther in their travels than the Greeks did. Also, the Greeks rarely mention the cat, considering it to be of little value.

Although cats may have been in Greece before Alexander the Great conquered that country in 332 B.C.E., the Archaic Greek word *gale* meant "weasel" or "polecat." Herodotus, Aristophanes, and Callimachus (fifth century B.C.E.) used the word *cattus* (cat), but very infrequently. Gale came to mean "cat" in post-classical Greek and is still used in that context today.

It wasn't until classical times that the cat was featured in art and literature in Greece. A bas-relief, dating from the Battle of Marathon in the fifth century B.C.E., shows a cat on a leash with its master.

However, there is a rock temple called *Speos Artemidos* (Cave of Artemis) that provides proof that the Greeks identified their goddess Artemis with the Egyptian Bast. Here were found many of the symbols used by Bast, such as statues and paintings of cats and drawings of the moon's phases. Some time in the earliest phase of their history, the Greeks adopted the goddess Artemis from older

Mid-Eastern cultures. As far back as 2,400 years ago, the Greek Artemis was associated with cats; as a beautiful and strong Moon deity, this goddess ruled over the protection of women and children, animals and their young.

Although there are wall paintings of cats in Etruscan cemeteries, Rome itself had little interest in the cat until the end of the Republic. Mosaics and paintings from Pompeii show cats in various actions with humans. In the ruins of this city, at least one woman's body was found cradling her pet cat.[6]

The later Romans very probably kept domesticated cats, because the Roman armies later took cats with them as far as Britain.[7] They also recognized the cat as an animal sacred to their Moon goddess Diana (a form of the Greek Artemis). Wherever the cult of Diana existed, her worshippers met four times a year at night in mountains, caves, or woodland places far from other people. Because these devotees used remnants of ancient Egyptian goddess rituals, and the Moon and cat symbols, they came to be called witches. They believed that Diana would appear if her name was called seven times at these rituals.[8]

The feline species *Felis silvestris* was known to the Gauls only as a ferocious wild animal. The domestic cat probably didn't arrive in the territory of the Gauls until around the fourth century C.E. However, the cat was considered a powerful totem among the Gaelic peoples. In Scotland, Caithness was named after the clan of Catti (cat people), while in Irish mythology, the hero Finn fought against a tribe of "cat-heads."[9] The warriors of the Irish king, known as Carbar of the Cat's Head, wore the skins of wild cats on their helmets.

In Scotland, when the harvest had been cut, a handful of grain or straw was left unbound in the field; this offering was called the "cat." In Bohemia they sometimes killed a cat and buried it in a cornfield to protect the crop. In other European countries, the person to cut the last of the grain was called the "tom-cat" or "she-cat."

No mention of the cat is recorded in India's history until after the second century B.C.E. The Sanskrit word for cat was *Margaras* (hunter, investigator).

Edward the Black Prince's crest, possibly a later version of the cat-head helmet

---

6. Roni Jay, *Mystic Cats.*
7. Cat paw prints have been found on Roman tiles in at least one of the British Roman ruins.
8. The ancient Egyptians held the same belief about Isis and Bast.
9. This possibly refers to warriors who wore catskins over their helmets; Katherine Briggs, *Dictionary of Fairies.*

Qetesh, an Egyptian Moon-goddess who stands upon a lion (from Budge's *The Gods of the Egyptians, Vol. 2*)

European writers don't mention the cat at all until the first century C.E. An Old English name for a tomcat was Gib or Gibbe-cat (hard g). By the tenth century, law in West Wales listed the cat with a definite monetary value. If a cat was killed, the offender had to replace it with a sheep and a lamb.

Clues to a Moon and cat worshipping practice remain in a strange runic wheel-cross built into a wall of a parish church on the Isle of Man. This wheel-cross, about four feet in diameter, is divided into four quarters. Three of the quarters contain images of cats, one lean, one normal, and one fat, while the fourth quarter has the outline of a shrew-mouse. On the upper arm of this cross are two cats, supporting a human face between them. According to Plutarch, a human face between two cats symbolized that the changes of the Moon were affected by wisdom and understanding.

At one time in European history, some ships were called cats, such as certain Norwegian vessels and the English flat-bottomed fire boats of 1804. Possibly this name was used because of the ancient idea that cats and priestesses who used the power of cats could control wind, storm, and waters.

There is only one known representation of a feline-headed female form in North America. About 1,100 years old, this amulet was found in a peat bog in Key Marco Island in Florida, and has been identified as having been part of the Native American Calusa culture in that region.

The Chinese, for some reason, did not attempt to domesticate the cat until about 200 to 400 C.E. Other Oriental cultures, such as Siam and Burma, valued certain cats or cats of certain breeds with special markings.[10]

The Oriental systems of astrology use animals to symbolize different years; by their calculation, they consider the year of birth to be important and don't use the monthly astrology signs known in the West. Suzanne White[11] writes that in Vietnam the cat replaces the Chinese rabbit. The last cycle of the Year of the Cat was in 1987.

---

10. There is one school of thought that believes Oriental cats originated in ancient Egypt and were taken to these areas in some manner.
11. *Book of Chinese Chance.*

Cats are infrequently used in heraldry and on coats of arms, but they do appear. On all the arms of France, Germany, Holland, and Italy, there are probably not a hundred that feature cats.

The first known heraldic cat was the red cat on the arms of the most famous Roman Legion—the *Felices seniores*. Another Legion had a banner with a green cat on a silver background, while a third carried a banner of a red cat on a pink shield. An alpine Roman troop bore the symbol of a cat with only one eye and one ear.

The cat is on the coat of arms of the clan Chattan of Scotland; the cat, and the motto "All by love, nothing by force," was on the blazon of the dukes of Bourgogne. Other European coats of arms featuring cats are Dekater, Platen, Kater, Brockman, Chazot, Katte of Vicritz, and Chaurand.

Examples of cats in heraldry

The domesticated cat has had a great many famous supporters and admirers through the centuries. Pope Leo XII had a tabby named Micetto, who was his constant companion. Thomas Wolsey (1471–1530) took his cat everywhere. The French cardinal Richelieu installed dozens of cats at the court. Queen

Marie Leczinska, wife of the French king Louis XV, loved cats so much that they were given the run of the city. Charles I of England had a black cat whom he adored. When the cat got sick and died, Charles I said his luck was gone; the next day he was arrested. The third Earl of Southampton was imprisoned in the Tower of London in the seventeenth century because he was suspected of treason; his cat climbed the Tower and entered his cell through a chimney to be with him.

In more recent history, felines have also found their friends. Abraham Lincoln found three little cats, almost dead with the cold, in General Grant's camp during the Civil War; he adopted them. Queen Victoria of England was a cat lover. During the London blitz, Winston Churchill always made certain that his ginger tom Jock was safe. Theodore Roosevelt wrote often about the antics of his two cats, Tom Quartz and Slippers (who had six toes). Harold Wilson, who had a Siamese named Nemo, and several of his cabinet members were also cat lovers. Louis Pasteur, Einstein, and Dr. Schweitzer all had cats; Schweitzer, who was left-handed, would use his right hand rather than disturb his cat Sizi. Even the dictator Mussolini and the Russian Nicholai Lenin loved cats. The writer Raymond Chandler often talked over his stories with his black Persian Taki.

An interesting footnote of history says that Sir Isaac Newton had several cats and was always concerned about their comfort. When he noticed that they were unhappy waiting for him to open the door for them, he invented the cat flap, which allowed the cats to come and go as they pleased.

Cats have also had their share of haters. Julius Caesar detested cats, as did Ambroise Pare, the surgeon to the court of Henri III of France. Henri himself fainted at the very sight of a cat. The eighteenth-century grand sultan of Turkey, Abdulhamid, was absolutely terrified of them. Napoleon was so paranoid about cats that he would break into a sweat and go berserk if the tiniest kitten came into his sight. The Frenchmen Voltaire and Georges Cuvier (zoologist) disliked cats immensely. And the English field marshall Lord F. S. Roberts swore he couldn't breathe if a cat was anywhere near him. The composer Johannes Brahms spent his leisure time shooting cats from his windows with a bow. Dwight Eisenhower gave orders that any cat seen on the grounds of his Gettysburg home was to be shot.

Superstitions

In ancient Egypt, women wore an amulet of a cat so they would be fortunate in love and all things feminine. A woman who wanted children would wear an amulet of a cat and kittens, the number of kittens indicating the number of children she wished to have.

Wives were once made to drink milk that held a cat's eye stone to prevent them conceiving children while the husband was gone on a journey.

If a black cat crosses your path or enters your house, it will bring good luck. This superstition may have come from ancient Egypt, where the sacred cats (and especially the black ones) were said to bring blessings on any house that took care of them. Egyptian tomb inscriptions have been found that say that the cat will give long life, prosperity, and good health.

You will be extremely rich or lucky in love if you pull off a white hair from a black cat without getting scratched (Lowlands of Brittany).

If a cat crosses your path and does you no harm, you will be very lucky. This superstition comes from medieval times, during the very era when the "devil cat" was so hated. Because the orthodox church could not peacefully separate the people from Goddess worship and the veneration of Her cats, they linked the cat with their devil. Obviously, this superstition is a twisted version of the older, less negative one.

If a black cat crosses your path, you will have good luck. The black cat is also considered to be an omen of money (England).

If a cat comes into your house, be kind to it, and the devil will not bother you.
Another medieval twist of the superstition, this also assumes that the cat and the devil are in league. By inference, if you have the devil on your side, he will go torment someone else.

Whenever the cat of the house is black, the lasses of lovers will have no lack.

If a cat sneezes, luck is coming to the house.

Keep an old cat collared and chained in a shop, and prosperity will be yours. If the cat escaped, the prosperity was believed to go with it (China).

In parts of Yorkshire the wives of fishermen keep black cats at home to ensure their husbands' safety at sea.

In southern England if a black cat crosses the path of a bride as she leaves church, it will be a fortunate marriage.
This is still a popular English belief. Like hiring a chimney sweep to give her a good luck kiss when she exits the church, the bride may also make arrangements to have a black cat led across her path.

If you have a white cat, silver will always be in the house. If you have a dark-colored cat, there will always be gold (an ancient Buddhist superstition).

A tortoiseshell cat brings good fortune (Ireland and Scotland).

A cat with three colors will protect your house against fire.

A cat insures its owner of good luck (China).

People who dislike cats will be carried to the cemetery through rain (Holland).

If you treat a cat badly or neglect it, carry an umbrella to your wedding (Holland).

Cats who have three colors (red, white, and black) are able to predict the approach of storms (Japan).

In many cultures, a sneezing cat means rain.

A wildly running and playful cat is a sign of an approaching storm.

When a cat washes behind its ears, it is pulling down rain.

If a ship's cat starts running and playing, it means a gale or wind behind them and rain in their faces (an old sailor's belief).

If a cat scratches a table leg, it means a change in the weather.

If a cat sits with its back to the fire, it means a storm is coming.

To decide whether to say yes or no to a marriage proposal, take three hairs from a cat's tail. Wrap them in white paper and put this under the doorstep overnight. In the morning carefully open the paper. If the hairs are in a Y-shape, it is yes; if in an N-shape, it is no (The Ozarks).

Cats will deliberately suffocate babies in their cribs. They will suck away the breath of any sleeping or ill person, leaving them weak or even killing them.
  This erroneous idea was developed during the witch-frenzy and, unfortunately, is still widely held by otherwise intelligent people. Some cats will sit on your chest and get close to your face because they want attention, but they have absolutely no need to suck away your breath.

Cats carry the souls of the dead to the afterworld (Finnish folklore).

If a cat jumps over a coffin, the soul of the deceased will not be able to find its way to heaven (Scotland).

To kill a black cat brings bad luck. Another version is you will get rheumatism if you kill a cat.

If a black cat crosses your path, you will have bad luck (America).
  In almost every country, except the U.S., Spain, and Belgium, the black cat is considered to be a lucky omen. It is strange that the bad press from the early orthodox church still affects the American way of thinking about black cats, but the Europeans have freed themselves from it.

If a cat jumps onto a pregnant woman, the unborn child will die (old Southern belief).

Miners won't say the word *cat* while underground. If a cat should appear in the mines, they will refuse to work until the cat is killed.

If you see a strange cat, it means changes in your life, while the sight of a black cat means misfortune or illness (China).

Lightning bolts are sent by angels to rid cats of the evil spirits that possess them, so put cats outside during a storm (Scotland and Slavic countries).

If a cat mews on board a ship, it is a sign of a troublesome voyage (Wales).

The eyes of cats shine in the dark.
The eyes of cats don't shine unless there is light to reflect in them. Witch hunters said this "night shine" reflection was the fires of hell and a sign that cats roamed the world carrying the devil's influence.

The eyes of a cat will wax and wane with the phases of the Moon.[12]
The Romans even believed that the cat's whole body was affected by the phases of the Moon,[13] with the body getting thinner or fatter along with the Moon.

Cats are extremely nervous.
Not so; they just have superb reflexes and are very sensitive to loud noises. Cats hear two octaves above human levels of hearing. Their ears are so sensitive that loud noises actually cause them pain.

Blood from the tail of a black cat will cure many minor illnesses if rubbed on the affected body part.[14]
One such disease said to be cured in this manner was shingles.

If a cat sneezes three times, everyone in the house will catch colds.
Many people still believe that humans can catch all kinds of dangerous diseases from cats when, in fact, this isn't true at all.

To cure any illness in a family, wash the patient and throw the water over a cat. Then drive the cat outside; it will take the illness with it.

---

12. Plutarch believed this, and W. B. Yeats wrote about it in his poem *The Cat & the Moon*.
13. Roni Jay, *Mystic Cats*.
14. This is a medical remedy from the time immediately after the witch hunts, when the church took away the power of the Pagan doctors (particularly the women doctors) and turned it over to "educated" men.

For a sty, stroke the eye with the tail of a black cat. Or pluck a hair from the tip of a black cat's tail when the New Moon rises on a cloudless day and draw the hair across the swollen eyelid nine times (Cornwall).

A similar belief is if you stroke the tail of a black cat across a wart during the month of May only, the wart will go away.

In early times in the southern U.S.A., it was believed that gravy made from a stewed cat would cure consumption.

If the cats desert a house, there will always be sickness there.

No cat that has been purchased will catch mice.

Cats born in May will only catch snakes and worms.

Don't feed a cat well if you want it to catch mice.
> This is a terrible belief, and erroneous too. The hunger of a cat has nothing to do with its hunting abilities. Most well-fed cats will hunt avidly simply because of their inborn instincts.

When moving, butter a cat's paws to make them stay at the new house.
> In fact, by the time the cat licked the butter off its paw it was fairly familiar with the new house. Actually, keeping an outside cat indoors for about a week and giving it a bag of fresh catnip will usually keep it from running away in fright. The idea is to let the cat get accustomed to the new place.

Boil the ear of a black cat in the milk of a black sow and wear it on your thumb to become invisible (Albertus Magnus).[15]

Wear a cat's (or tiger's) eye stone to become invisible (Arabia).

Wearing a cat's eye stone will return the evil eye to the sender (Medieval times).

---

15. This magician was the teacher of St. Thomas Aquinas; Miles Abelard, *Physicians of No Value.*

In the Ozarks and other parts of the southern U.S.A, if a cat washes itself while sitting in a doorway, a member of the clergy will soon arrive. If it only washes its left ear, a female visitor is on the way; if only the right ear, it will be a male visitor.

A cat ensures its owner of good luck (China).

4

Feline Deities

A great many deities around the world and in various cultures have been connected in one way or another with the feline family. Perhaps the best known are the Egyptian goddesses Bast and Sekhmet and the Norse goddess Freyja. But the

It is in their eyes that their magic resides.

—ARTHUR SYMONS

spiritual importance of all cats and their connection to deities reached back much further than ancient Egypt.

Paleolithic art tells us that the lion once roamed over much of Europe. Sacred caves are decorated with detailed paintings of the slaying of lions. The very fact that these paintings are in such detail and in such sacred places hints that the slaying was more than a mere hunt, possibly of great religious significance.[1] We know that such caves were symbolic of the body of the Great Goddess,[2] the resting place between death and rebirth.

In the huge cave of Pech Merle in France is a painting of a red human-lion figure, wearing a crown; called the Lion Queen,[3] this has been the only one of its kind found thus far. In the foothills of the Pyrenees is a cave (Les Trois Freres) containing the Chapel of the Lioness; on a stone altar is carved a lioness and her cub. This lioness has been termed the Guardian of Initiation.[4]

From a later date (1800 B.C.E.) in Iran, we find a golden bowl engraved with the Mother Goddess and Her lions. Wearing two necklaces (symbol of fertility), She rides a lion, while holding a mirror (the Sun) in one hand and a mace (thunderbolt) in the other. On the lion's flank is a swastika, an ancient sacred fertility symbol before it was perverted by Hitler.

The Hittites of the Middle East, of whom we know little, also connected the Great Goddess and the lion. On a high plateau in Turkey are the ruins of the Hittite capital Yasilakaya; it was destroyed in c. 1200 B.C.E. by invaders from the Black Sea region.[5]

It wasn't until the nineteenth century C.E. that a French traveler discovered a hidden sacred sanctuary in a rocky gorge about two miles from the ancient ruins. Inside, in a series of rock chambers, are almost seventy huge human and divine figures. In the center of this group of sculptures are seven deities on their respective sacred animals. The most important of this grouping is the Storm and Weather God, standing on the shoulders of two retainers, and the Great Goddess, who rides a lion. These statues likely represent the well-documented Sumerian-Babylonian Sacred Marriage, considered so very important for the welfare of the realm.

A lion architectural ornament from Nineveh and Persepolis

Several representations of lions with the Goddess have been found in the ancient ruins of Crete and Mycenae. For example, a seal ring from Crete shows a Great Goddess figure standing between two guardian lions as She gestures with a

1. Buffie Johnson, *Lady of the Beasts*.
2. Erich Neumann, *The Great Mother*.
3. Siegfried Giedion, *The Eternal Present*.
4. Ibid.
5. Gertrude R. Levy, *The Sword from the Rock*.

©1984 Michele & Tom Grimm/International Stock

Bronze lion guarding the Gate of Supreme Harmony in Beijing, China

wand. At the entrance to the acropolis of Mycenae (1250 B.C.E.) is the famous Lion Gate; here, two lions, carved in deep relief, guard a Goddess pillar.

A bronze relief from 500 B.C.E. was discovered in the Etruscan area of Italy. On it is the Gorgon Medusa, shown in the birth position and flanked by two lionesses, which she holds by the throats. This depiction is reminiscent of those found at Catal Huyuk in Turkey.

The goddess Cybele, who was worshipped in Phrygia, Thrace, Lydia, Phoenicia, and many other places, first is shown standing between two lions; later, in Spartan art, she stands on a lion or holds one by the throat. Much later, the Roman Goddess Fortuna sits in a chariot pulled by lions, while in India and Tibet, the goddess Tara rides on a lion. The Homeric hymn to Aphrodite says that this deity was accompanied by grim-eyed lions and fleet leopards.

In China, the lion (called *Shih*) was one of the four animals of power.[6] It was said to watch over and protect the living and the dead, as well as magickally call forth rain. Even today in the U.S.A., many Chinese perform lion dances before their homes to the accompaniment of drums and firecrackers.[7]

---

6. Alfred Salmony, *Antler & Tongue.*
7. After lions became extinct in China, the Pekingese dog was specially bred to resemble the lion. These same animals became guardians.

However, lions were not the only member of the feline family to have ancient spiritual significance. At the ancient ruins of the matriarchal Turkish city of Catal Huyuk (7100–6300 B.C.E.) is a three-dimensional sculpture of a goddess dressed in spotted leopard skins and riding a leopard.[8] Another discovery from Catal Huyuk is a terra-cotta figure of a Mother Goddess sitting on a birth-throne; between Her ample thighs is the head of the partially born child.[9] Her hands rest on the heads of leopards. Thousands of similar terra cottas are now in the Ankara Architectural Museum in Turkey. Among these figures are also statues of men wearing leopard skins and dancing in rituals.

In the neighboring ruins of Halicar (c. 6000 B.C.E.) there is archaeological evidence that similar religious practices were used. Among the clay figures is one of the Mother Goddess, less ample than those of Catal Huyuk, with elongated eyes; She sits on a throne with a leopard as guard, while She nurses a leopard cub.[10]

In the far north in the Scandinavian countries, we find a few representations of the goddess Freyja and her two cats, who were said to pull her chariot. Her priestesses were known to wear cat-skin capes and gloves during rituals.

These are just a few of the numerous archaeological, historical, and written examples of ancient spiritual connections between felines and deities, particularly goddesses. Although the connection between felines and deities is widespread, present-day readers are mainly familiar with the Egyptian connections, particularly the goddesses Bast and Sekhmet.

Certain Egyptian deities have long been associated with the feline family and its powers. A crystal cup from 3100 B.C.E. is engraved with a picture of the lion-headed goddess Mafdet. Papyri from later times portray the Sun god Ra in giant cat form, a knife in one paw, beheading the serpent Apep. The Egyptians named the cat after its own speech: Mau.[11] Several of the royal tombs of the Nineteenth and Twentieth Dynasties of Thebes are decorated with the words of the Seventy-Five Praises of Ra; one of these Praises calls Ra the Great Cat, the judge of words.[12]

However, the goddess Bast was frequently called "the eye of Ra," a clue that she alone was originally the Great Cat and that this title was later given to the god.

---

8. James Mellaart, *Catal Huyuk.*
9. Ibid.
10. James Mellaart, *Excavations at Hacilar.*
11. Budge, *The Gods of the Egyptians.*
12. Ibid.

The principal Egyptian goddesses associated with the domestic cat were Bast and Pasht.[13] They both were pictured with a human female body and the head of a cat. Bast represented the gentler aspects of the cat, while Pasht symbolized the aggressive aspects.

The idea of the cat and its nine lives may have come from an Egyptian belief that the goddess Pasht had nine lives; the Egyptian Ennead was also made up of nine deities. The number nine has been associated with the Moon in many ancient cultures since the earliest of times. The Greek/Roman goddess Artemis/Diana, who was identified with Bast, was also associated with the number nine (the nine Muses), the Moon, and the cat; the priestesses of Diana were often masked and robed to resemble cats.

The Egyptians who were educated and initiated into the Mysteries never actually worshipped any animal as an animal. Instead, they honored the animal as an incarnation or representation of a divine presence or deity.[14]

Bast, or Bastet or Ubastet, was a goddess greatly loved by the ancient Egyptians. Her name may have come from the Egyptian word *bes*, which means "fire." Called the Cat Mother and the Little Cat, she was connected primarily with the Moon (as well as the Sun) and domesticated cats, and often called the "eye of the Moon."[15]

The Cat Ra cutting the snake as depicted in the Papyrus of Hu-nefer

13. A few writers believe that the cat was connected with the dark god Set, but this isn't consistent with Egyptian records.
14. Budge, *Egyptian Magic.*
15. Lurker, *The Gods & Symbols of Ancient Egypt.*

Her most famous temple was at Bubastis-Aboo-Pahst,[16] in the Delta region. At Thebes and Heliopolis, Bast also held a greatly honored position. She is mentioned in the *Pyramid Texts* but only occasionally in the *Egyptian Book of the Dead*. The worship of Bast was already very old when the name of Pepi I of the Fifth Dynasty was entered in her temple at Bubastis.

Priestesses and women honored Bast with music, dance, merrymaking, and sexual rites. Sistra[17] used by her priestesses and worshippers were decorated with the head or image of a cat at the top. Known as the "lady of Sept" (the star of Sothis), Bast was called the bringer of good fortune.

However, the seventeenth chapter of the *Egyptian Book of the Dead* hints that Bast had much more serious duties than revelry; she knew certain powerful words that would banish the powers of all darkness.

The black cat, associated with both Bast and Pasht, was thought to be especially lucky and was the emblem used by physicians to advertise their services.

A similar goddess to Bast, and with many of the same aspects, was Hathor, called the Lioness. The connection between these two goddesses is shown by an inscription of Ramses IV that said that hunting lions was forbidden on the festival of Bast. Hathor, in her aspect of the Eye of Ra, was frequently accompanied by Bast and Sekhmet.

In the tale of Isis and the child Horus, found in the *Egyptian Book of the Dead*, Isis herself says that Horus is nursed by the cat who dwells in the House of Neith (Neith was a goddess).

Although desert and red-colored animals were ordinarily considered sacred to the god Set, this did not apply to lions, cheetahs, cats, and other members of the feline family. Most Egyptian deities associated with the lion (a solar animal) were goddesses. Gateways to temples, palaces, and tombs, as well as the royal throne itself, were guarded by images of the lion.[18] The head of the funeral bier was carved in the shape of a lion's head, a symbolic reminder that lion-headed deities guarded certain halls of the Underworld. One of the oldest human-headed lion statues is the famous Sphinx at Gizeh.[19]

---

16. Budge, *The Gods of the Egyptians*, and M. Oldfield Howey, *The Cat in Magic*. Herodotus wrote that this temple was specifically built to honor Bast.
17. Sistrum is the singular; sistra is the plural.
18. Originally, the home of the Egyptian lion was the Delta and the jungles of the Blue Nile river. It was also found in the deserts on both sides of the Nile between Khartum and the Mediterranean Sea, although not in great numbers.
19. Budge, *The Gods of the Egyptians*.

©Aldo Sessa/International Stock

One of the oldest human-headed lion statues is the famous Sphinx;
this photo depicts one in Karnak, Egypt

Ancient records tell us that lions were kept as sacred animals in many temples and palaces throughout Egypt, particularly in the temple at Heliopolis. Ramses II and III both had a tame lion who attacked the enemy during battle.

The Egyptian goddess Sekhmet is mentioned in the Pyramid Texts, was associated with the lioness, and was worshipped at Beni Hasan. Called "the night huntress with the sharp claws," she was portrayed with a lioness head, representing the devouring heat of the Sun. As a deity of fertility, she protected the young; she was also associated with fate, because she ruled over the Tablets of Destiny, and also with war and destruction.

Sekhmet's name, which means "the mighty one; the strong, violent; the tearer and devourer of men," seems to be derived from the root *sekhem*. She was also known as the Great Cat.[20] As a powerful goddess who protected the good and destroyed the evil, she could defeat the powers of Set and the serpent Apophis. Her festival day commemorated the massacre of humans by Sekhmet as the Great Cat. Both Bast and the goddess Sekhmet were considered to be protectors of the Sun god and destroyers of his enemies.

Another of her lesser-known symbols was the fire-spitting uraeus (cobra). Statues of Sekhmet often wore a crown of the uraeus and Sun disk, while the goddess herself was draped in a red garment.

The Egyptians called Sekhmet "the one great of magick," a goddess who had access to knowledge of all sorcery. With her husband Ptah and her son Nefer-Tem, Sekhmet made up the deity triad of Memphis. The Greeks knew this goddess as Sakhmis.

When the Egyptian people wanted a goddess to protect them, they called upon Sekhmet. When they wanted more personal, gentle aid, they called upon Bast.

Bast was also shown on occasion with a lioness head. This makes Bast look very much like Sekhmet and makes it difficult to distinguish between the two. However, Neville Langton, an Egyptologist, studied these two goddesses and discovered a way to tell them apart when Bast wore her lioness form. Sekhmet almost always wore both the solar disk and uraeus, while Bast wore only the cobra-crown. Bast also carried the sistrum and had engraved between her ears the sign of the scarab. The sacred eye of Horus often was found somewhere on statues of Bast.

Like Sekhmet, the goddess Mehit was connected with the lioness. She was also identified with the fire-spitting uraeus (cobra), called the eye of Ra.

---

20. Patricia Dale-Green, *Cult of the Cat*.

Other Egyptian lioness-goddesses were Pakheth, Menat, Renenet, Sebqet, Urt-Hekau, Asthertet, and a form of Hathor and Nekhebet.[21] Even the South Wind was said to be ruled over by a lion-headed god called Shehbui.

The goddess Mafdet was associated with both the lynx[22] and the leopard or panther. Mafdet's claws were said to be like the spear of the god Horus; one of her sacred emblems was the execution pole, a device with a projecting blade at the top. Although she wreaked terror on evildoers, she also helped the dead in the Judgment Hall. The priests who officiated in the Opening of the Mouth ceremony for the dead wore panther skins. Mafdet was also called on for protection against snakes.

The worship of Bast had its followers throughout the Mediterranean area until the end of the fourth century c.e., when the Christian-backed emperor Theodosius I outlawed all Paganism.

After the frenzied paranoia of the witch hunts faded away, the church conveniently began to include the cat in its religious paintings. Unfortunately, the cat was usually portrayed in a negative sense, such as sitting at the feet of Judas in paintings of the Last Supper.

Greek legend says that the goddess Artemis (Diana) turned herself into a cat when fleeing from the evil god Typhon; in this same flight, the goddess Hecate also assumed a cat form. Because Hecate was associated with cats, the pussy willow, which bears "catkins" in the spring, was one of her plants.[23]

Cats are companion figures in many sculptures of the Roman Moon goddess Diana. The Roman goddess Liberty also was portrayed with a cat at her feet.

The black cat is especially associated with Underworld goddesses, such as the Norse

21. Budge, *The Gods of the Egyptians.*
22. The Egyptian word for lynx was Mafet; Ibid. The lynx attacked and killed snakes, a common danger in Egypt.
23. Robert Graves, *The Greek Myths.*

Hel, the Germanic Holda, and the Greek Hecate. This may be the reason that some people consider the black cat to be an omen of death.

Dionysus receiving his cat-skin

The Greek Sun god Apollo Chrysocomes (He of the Golden Locks) was sometimes identified with the lion and its flowing mane.

In Greek art, the tiger is sometimes substituted for the leopard in depictions of the god Dionysus. Legend isn't very clear about whether the newborn Dionysus was placed by Hermes on the skin of a leopard, a tiger, or a fawn.

In Mediterranean cultures, the goddess Cybele and her son/lover Attis rode in a lion-drawn chariot.

Early Arabs had a deity called Yaghuth, a lion god, and considered the lion a protector against evil.

The goddess Ishtar of Babylon was often shown standing on a lion or with two lions. For Marduk, a Sumerian god, the lion symbolized sovereignty and strength. In Chaldea, Nergal, the god of war and death, was often pictured as a lion. Among the Hittites, their weather god's chariot was pulled by lions and their Great Mother rode a lioness. At different times in Babylon and Assyria, the lion was connected with Ningirsu, Ninlil, Ninurta, Ishtar, Inanna, Astarte, and Damkina.

The most important goddess of the Norse cultures was Freyja, daughter of the sea god Njord and sister of Freyr. Her place in Asgard was called Folkvangr and her hall Sessrumnir. Freyja's chariot was pulled by two cats;[24] when the god Balder was cremated, she rode to the event in her cat-drawn chariot. This goddess liked love songs and helped in finding love; however, she was not associated with marriage.[25]

The Northern European Corn Cat, a deity called on to protect the crops, could well be a form of Freyja. In some parts of Europe today, country people still dress up as cats to celebrate the end of the harvest.

---

24. Turville-Petre, *Myth & Religion of the North*. Branston, *Gods of the North*.

25. Like Diana and other goddesses associated with the Moon and cats, the patriarchal Christians said that Freyja was the mistress of evil, a cohort of their devil. Since the followers of Moon goddesses often celebrated joyous sexual rites, the church felt obligated to persecute them; to them, sex was sinful, especially if women were free to indulge in it whenever they wanted.

Freyja and her cat-drawn chariot

After the people converted to Christianity, Freyja became a witch and her cats became black horses possessed by the devil. This new legend said that after seven years the cat-horses earned the right to become witches disguised as black cats. This rewrite of the Norse goddess story may be the origin of the unlucky black cat superstition. Those who accepted the idea of the Christian devil could also be persuaded to fear black cats.

Even the Celtic peoples, who viewed any cat as dangerous, had goddesses who could temporarily assume the form of a cat. Black Annis, a Crone aspect of the Great Goddess, was said to be able to shapeshift into a cat when she wanted to. When she was in this form, Black Annis had huge, sharp teeth and long nails or claws. She roamed the land at night, terrifying and killing people. In Scotland, the Cailleach Bheur (Blue Hag of Winter) could also become a cat. Reborn each year on October 31 (Halloween) and turned to stone on April 30, the Cailleach Bheur brought the freezing winter and snow.

In India, the Hindu goddess Shasti, deity of birth, either rode or was pictured with a cat, symbolizing the power of fertility and procreation. The goddess Durga was represented by a lion in her capacity of destroyer of demons; Durga also rode a tiger. The Hindu god Shiva, in his destructive aspect, wears a tiger skin.

The Chinese said that the cat was a yin animal connected with evil, the night, and shapeshifting. They believed that the appearance of a strange cat portended a change in fortune and that a black cat meant sickness and misfortune.

Tsai Shen, the Chinese god of wealth, rides a tiger who guards the money chests. In this aspect, the tiger becomes an emblem of gamblers. The goddess of wind also rides upon a tiger.

Unless otherwise stated, the designation of "cats" means cats in general.

Deities with Feline Associations

Deity (origin, gender)	Feline Association
Ahriman (Persia; god)	cats
Anait (Phoenicia, Canaan, Ur; goddess)	lion
Apollo (Greece; god)	lion
Artemis (Greece; goddess)	cats
Attis (Middle East; god)	lion
Bacchus (Rome; god)	panther
Bast (Egypt; goddess)	cats, lynx
Cybele (Greece, Phrygia; goddess)	lion
Damkina/Damgalnuna (Mesopotamia; goddess)	lion

Diana (Rome; goddess)	cats
Dionysus (Greece; god)	cheetah, lion, leopard, panther, tiger
Durga (India; goddess)	lion, tiger
Enki (Middle East; god)	lion
Freyja (Norse; goddess)	cats
Hathor (Egypt; goddess)	cat, lion
Horus (Egypt; god)	cats
Inanna (Canaan, Phoenicia, Sumeria, Uruk, Babylon; goddess)	lion
Ishtar (Mesopotamia, Babylon, Assyria, Sumeria, Arabia, Phoenicia, Canaan; goddess)	lion
Isis (Egypt; goddess)	cats
Liberty (Rome; goddess)	cats
Maat (Egypt; goddess)	lynx
Marduk (Mesopotamia; god)	lion
Mithras (Persia; god)	lion
Mut (Egypt; goddess)	lioness, cats
Nekhebet (Egypt; goddess)	lion
Nergal (Middle East, Babylon; god)	lion
Ningirsu (Middle East; god)	lion
Ninlil/Belitis (Mesopotamia; goddess)	lion
Ninurta (Mesopotamia; god)	lion
Osiris (Egypt; god)	leopard
Ovinnik (Slavonic; god)	black cats

Eros riding a lion

Pan (Greece; god)	leopard, panther
Pasht (Egypt; goddess)	cats
Ra (Egypt; god)	cats
Renenet (Egypt; goddess)	lion
Sakkan (Mesopotamia; god)	lion, cheetah, lynx, leopard
Sekhmet (Egypt; goddess)	lion, lioness
Set (Egypt; god)	cats
Shadrafa (Phoenicia; god)	lion
Shasti (India; goddess)	cats
Shiva (India; god)	tiger

Pan with one of his cats

Sacred Breeds and Temple Lore

Several specific breeds of cat were connected with ancient temples and sacred lore. Among those that readily come to mind are the Birman, the Siamese, and the black cats of ancient Egypt.

The smallest feline is a masterpiece.

—**Leonardo da Vinci**

Egyptian wall paintings of 3,000 to 4,000 years ago show cats with light or washed-out, broken tabby stripes, very similar to the present-day African wild cat. A painting of a cat wearing a wide collar is shown as early as the Fifth Dynasty (c. 2600 B.C.E.) in Egypt; this is in the tomb of Ti. A tomb picture from the Eighteenth Dynasty (c. 1400 B.C.E.) shows a cat in a papyrus swamp.[1] From the age of the New Kingdom (1567 B.C.E. onward), there are many paintings of cats sitting under chairs, hunting birds, and in the company of other tame animals. From the Tenth Dynasty on, the cat was frequently shown in Egyptian art. The cat would have been a welcome creature in any Egyptian

home regardless of its sacred designation because of the numerous rats, mice, snakes, and other dangerous Nile wildlife.

By 2100 B.C.E., close to the end of the Middle Empire, the Egyptians had trained the cat as a fisher and a hunter, as well as a ratter. Cats are shown in skiffs with hunters watching ducks and other water birds. One painting shows a cat holding down three birds, while another cat skillfully fishes beside it.

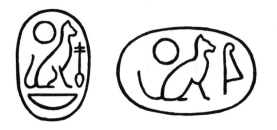

Cats were often featured in Egyptian hieroglyphics

An Egyptian tomb painting from the Nineteenth Dynasty pictures a deceased woman beside an offering table, with three animal deities hovering nearby: a cat, dog, and snake. This indicates that the cat in some manner was connected with the Egyptian belief in the afterlife. The most beautiful reproductions of cats are found in the tomb of the sculptors Apuki and Nebanin, who lived during the reign of Amen Hotep III.

By the Twentieth Dynasty, the cat held a strong place in Egyptian culture. They called the cat "Mau" or "Myeo," a name derived from the cat's meow. Even the poorest Egyptian willingly shared his meager meal with his cat.

The Egyptian sacred temple cats, as well as those of Babylon, were believed to act as the host for a human soul; this same belief was found much later among the Burmese and Siamese. Any human soul blessed by co-existing with a sacred cat would gain a high spiritual level when the cat finally died.

The city of Bubastis was founded in the Twenty-second Dynasty, when peace and prosperity were temporarily restored to Egypt.[2] During this period, the cat began to watch over temples, a task formerly reserved for lionesses.

The cat-headed goddess Bast or Bastet was a deity of maternity and all feminine things. The domestic cat became her special animal, and was deeply honored in her city of Bubastis. Cats were also sacred to her mirror-sister Pasht. In the temples of Bast-Pasht, the priests carefully watched the behavior and attitude of the cats living there; they gave predictions by the changes in behavior and actions.[3]

---

1. Champfleury, who wrote *Les Chats* in 1870, and others have traced domestic cats back to the Eighteenth Dynasty in Egypt.
2. Bubastis was built in Lower Egypt on the east branch of the Nile, a branch now silted up. Today this site is called Tell Basta.
3. Fernand Mery, *The Life, History & Magic of the Cat.*

All Egyptians, royalty and commoner alike, could have a cat. They revered cats so much that there was a death penalty for anyone who killed one. When a cat died, the family shaved off their eyebrows and went into mourning. Depending on their financial status, the family would embalm or bury the deceased cat.

The city of Bubastis, sacred to the cat goddess Bast, was the burial place of hundreds of thousands of mummified cats during the ancient Egyptian culture. These cats were carefully preserved, their eyes piously closed, wrapped in linen bandages, then buried in special cemeteries.

During the middle of the nineteenth century the sacred cat cemetery at Beni-Hassan was excavated. Unfortunately, both early archaeologists and the later Egyptian people themselves seemed to think these mummified remains were of no importance. In the late 1800s, boatloads of mummified cats[4] were taken to Europe, where the vast majority of them were pulverized and used as fertilizer. The Egyptologist Flinders Petrie himself gave 190 cat skulls to the English Natural History Museum. The three largest skulls have been identified as belonging to the jungle or marsh cat, *Felis chaus.*

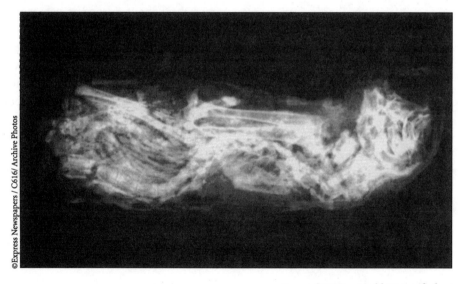

©Express Newspapers / C616/ Archive Photos

X-ray of 2,500-year-old mummified cat

---

4. In fact, twenty tons of these bodies were shipped to Liverpool, England, alone. Farmers bought them for £4 a ton.

The origin of the black cat can be traced back to ancient Egypt, where it (as were all cats) was considered especially sacred to the goddess Bast. Bast was often portrayed as a black cat. The black cat's European reputation for bringing good luck and healing comes from the ancient Egyptians' reverence for this cat.[5] For centuries, a pure black cat could be sold for a huge sum, equivalent to many thousands of dollars today.

The Phoenicians, who were the shady used horse- and car-dealers of the era, decided to trade in cats, a rare commodity and one the Egyptians firmly refused to sell to them or anyone else. Black cats were extremely rare, as most Egyptian cats were of a reddish, fawn, or yellowish color. The Phoenicians managed to steal a few of the sacred cats and sneak them out of Egypt,[6] roaming great distances along their trade routes; ancient tales from Britain and western France say that these seafarers brought rare cats with them from the Mediterranean.

In order to increase their product, the Phoenicians began to breed the cats. Soon they discovered that, although all their cats were valuable, the black ones brought the highest prices. They sold cats all around the Mediterranean, first in Greece and then on to Rome. However, they advertised the black cats as the most efficient mousers because their coloring made them almost invisible in the dark.

Later, the domesticated cat spread throughout Europe as pets were taken along with the Roman families to new colonies. In these new European areas, the domesticated cat encountered the European wild cat and began to interbreed. The resulting offspring produced the first full tabby coats with thin, dark lines.

The present-day Abyssinian cat has the look and reddish color of some of the cats pictured in Egyptian paintings. There are two groups of thought about the origin of the Abyssinian cat. One group thinks that the Abyssinian is descended from Egyptian sacred cats, which were worshipped more than 4,000 years ago. The other group thinks the breed originated in the jungles of North Africa. Both agree that the Abyssinian was brought to England during the late 1860s by soldiers returning from that area of the world.

Several centuries into the Common Era, Asian countries began to import domestic cats. India was the first of the Asian area to include the cat in its religion. For a very long time, Orthodox Hindu rites have stipulated that each family should care for at least one cat.

---

5. The black cat's healing powers were connected with the goddess Pasht, the mirror-sister of Bast.
6. The Egyptians prevented this export of cats for at least a thousand years after they accepted them as sacred pets. In fact, records hint that the Egyptians brought back to Egypt any cats they found during their travels.

No one definitely knows the origin of the Siamese cat. It may have been established by Pradgadipok, the father of a Siamese king. Pradgadipok confined his cats to his palace and guarded them. The boys who guarded these cats ignored the death penalty and occasionally stole one from a new litter, selling the kitten in Shanghai to tourists. The first Siamese pair reached England in 1884, the same year a pair showed up in France. The first Blue Point Siamese was bred in England in 1894, and the first Chocolate Point was a male brought to England in 1897.

At one time Siamese cats were noted for the kink in their tails.[7] The legend behind this is a quite charming story. The royal princesses of Siam needed some place safe to leave their rings when they went each day to bathe, so they slipped the rings over the tails of their Siamese cats. The cats, to keep from losing the rings, kinked their tails to keep the jewelry from slipping off. Thus the kink became permanent in the tails of Siamese cats.

Another tale of the kink says that the Siamese once tied a knot in its tail to remember something, but forgot what it was.

Another delightful tale of the Siamese explains the crossed eyes, once common but now rare. The crossed eyes, legend says, came from the diligent concentration of certain Siamese cats who were set the task of watching and guarding a certain sacred vase.

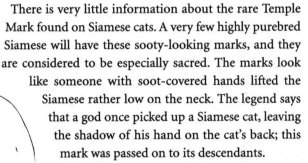

There is very little information about the rare Temple Mark found on Siamese cats. A very few highly purebred Siamese will have these sooty-looking marks, and they are considered to be especially sacred. The marks look like someone with soot-covered hands lifted the Siamese rather low on the neck. The legend says that a god once picked up a Siamese cat, leaving the shadow of his hand on the cat's back; this mark was passed on to its descendants.

Another Asian/Oriental cat is the Birman, which is the sacred cat of Burma and is a different breed from the Burmese cat. It was greatly honored in Burma because of the Burmese legend saying that deceased priests

---

7. Siamese are now bred for straight tails in the U.S. and Britain. However, in the Orient, kinked-tailed Siamese are valued. Milo Denlinger, *The Complete Siamese Cat.*

returned to their temples in the form of these cats. These sacred longhaired cats lived in certain holy places, one of which was the temple of Lao-Tsun, on the side of the mountain Lugh. This temple was located in west Burma between China and India.

Long ago, a priest named Kittah Mun-Ha lived in this temple. He was a great, pious Lama with a golden beard. Each night he would kneel in worship before a statue of Tsun-Kyan-Kse, the blue-eyed goddess who ruled over the transmutation of souls, a process that allows a spiritual person to relive the span of his next life within the body of a sacred animal. Each time Mun-Ha prayed, he was joined by a sacred cat named Sinh, a golden-eyed cat with white fur and dark-colored ears, tail, nose, and paws.

One night invaders from Siam stormed the temple, and Mun-Ha was killed. Immediately, the cat Sinh stood with his paws on the dead Mun-Ha and faced the statue of the goddess. As he stared at the statue, a wonderful transformation took place. The cat's fur changed to a beautiful golden color down his spine, while his feet remained a brilliant white; this white showed the purity of Mun-Ha's soul. Sinh's yellow eyes changed to a deep, sapphire blue. For seven days the sacred cat remained at his post before the statue. At the end of that time Sinh died, taking with him the soul of the priest Mun-Ha. When Sinh died, all the sacred cats in the temple were transformed from their original white color to that of the seal point, just like Sinh.

During a rebellion in Burma in 1916, a British officer, Major Gordon Russel, helped some of the priests escape to Tibet with their sacred Birman cats. The priests sent Major Russel a pair of Birman cats in gratitude.

The first Burmese cat (not the same as the Birman) arrived in the U.S. in 1930. She was a brown female named Wong Mau. Her owner, Dr. G. C. Thompson of San Francisco, mated her with a Siamese.

From about the time Buddhism was introduced to Japan (c. sixth century C.E.), there have been at least two cats in every Buddhist temple. This action was primarily taken to protect the manuscripts of moral treatises from being chewed up by mice.

Cats in Japan were considered so valuable that they were pampered and kept indoors; only the wealthy could afford to purchase a cat. The example for this devotion may have been the Emperor himself. In 999 C.E., a white cat brought from China gave birth to five white kittens in the court at Kyoto. The Emperor decreed that these cats would be brought up and protected as if they were young princes.

It wasn't until centuries later that the cat was allowed outside, and it became possible for the lower ranks of citizens to have a cat. In 1602 the destruction of silkworms by mice reached a danger point. The Japanese government passed a law that all adult cats had to be set free so they could kill the mice. It was forbidden to even buy, sell, or make a gift of a cat.

Today, deceased cats have their own temple, Gotoku-Ji in Tokyo, built about 200 years ago. This charming temple is still served by priests wearing sacred gar-

A Japanese
bamboo stencil

ments and chanting for the cat souls buried there. On the altar at the heart of this temple are many portrayals of cats on paper and cloth, in porcelain and bronze. Each of them is shown with an upraised paw, raised to the heighth of its eyes.[8] This peculiar position represents Maneki-Neki, the little female cat who is thought to attract good luck and happiness. Around this altar are the graves of beloved cats, all covered with tablets on which are inscribed prayers to Buddha for their souls.

Originally, the temple of Gotoku-Ji was only a poor thatched hut run by poverty-stricken Buddhist monks. The head priest, however, had a little cat with whom he shared his meager food. Wishing to help the monks, the cat went to the roadside one day and waited until a troop of Samurai came riding down the road. The cat raised its paw to its ear as if beckoning, and the curious Samurai

8. This "beckoning" cat is considered to be a powerful good luck charm that draws prosperity. A figure of this cat often decorates the entrances to Japanese shops and restaurants.

stopped to look at the cat. As the cat continued to beckon and move closer to the poor temple, the men followed.

The head priest gave them tea and talked about the Buddhist doctrine as a heavy rainstorm kept the men inside. After this, one of the Samurai, Lord Li, regularly visited the priest to hear about Buddhism. He finally endowed the temple with a large estate, which is the Gotoku-Ji temple of today.

In China, the god of agriculture was Li-Shou, who was worshipped in the form of a cat. After the harvest was reaped and stored, the people made sacrifices to this god so that, in his cat form, he would protect against rats and mice. A parallel European minor deity was very similar: known as the Corn Cat, this deity had both a human and a cat shape and was linked with good harvests and protection of crops.

There is no definite way to determine exactly where the cat first became considered sacred, although archaeology points to ancient Egypt. However much methods of spirituality changed over the centuries, the cat remained mysterious, mystical, and sacred to one degree or another among a great many cultures. The cat has been considered a powerful totem animal or familiar in several religious paths. Perhaps those people who seem to enjoy harming or torturing cats today are reacting to the subconscious knowledge that the feline family was once of great importance in guiding humans along a positive spiritual path, and that they still hold that power.

6

The Persecution of Cats

Cats in general have succumbed to some of the most hideous, nasty persecutions ever perpetrated on an animal. This torture and murder was done in the name of religion, and the black cat received the worst of the treatment. Even today, cat owners should beware around Halloween time, especially if they have a black cat. Such cats frequently become the target for mistreatment or death.

> Cats are a mysterious kind of folk. There is more passing in their minds than we are aware of.
>
> —Sir Walter Scott

Unfortunately, there are still people today who feel they should not be punished for torturing cats. In a recent news story, a science teacher in Braggs, Oklahoma, tried to force his students to remove the kidney of a stray cat. When the poor cat came out of the anesthetic during the procedure and started crying, the teacher walked out of the room, leaving the students to sew up the incision. One of the students took the cat immediately to a vet and then home to live. Students complained to the SPCA and the police, who were then forced to do something because of the

publicity. When the teacher was cited with only a misdemeanor and given a $500 fine, local people raised the money, and the school board kept him on with no punishment whatsoever.[1] However, torturing cats has become repugnant to enough other people that some states, such as Pennsylvania, are passing strong laws against such criminal acts.[2]

In the very beginning of Christianity, there was really no trouble over cats. The church ignored the cat completely because of its association with Pagan religions; for example, the cult of Artemis (Diana), a goddess whom the church later taught was the consort of their devil. In fact, the church preached that witches and witchcraft were a fantasy product only of the mind.

There was no great problem about "devil" cats doing foul deeds for the Christian devil until medieval times. By the thirteenth century, people had lost so much faith in the Christian structure that the church began to look for a scapegoat and settled on witchcraft. The churches began to preach against the cat as a minion of their devil Satan, and anyone who associated lovingly with a cat was condemned as well.[3] They declared the cat, particularly the black cat, to be associated with the foul rites of black magic and sorcery.

The term "witch" was applied to anyone who still believed in a Pagan religion as opposed to Christianity, especially women. The old Pagan religions honored women and allowed them to be priestesses, two things the church was against. Because the cat, owl, bat, hare, and wolf were animals of the Great Goddess, Christianity linked them with "witches" (priestesses and Pagan women). People came to believe that witches were automatically evil, and so were the animals linked with the Goddess.

Many people even believed that a witch could take on the form of a cat nine times during her lifetime.[4] The image of a black cat flying through the night sky on a broomstick came from the same era. In Hungary, it was said that all cats between the ages of seven and

---

1. Spring 1996 *Quarterly Journal of the National Humane Education Society.*
2. It has been my personal observation that humans who torture cats have the capacity to do (and often do) the same to other animals and humans, especially spouses and children. This Pennsylvania law is ironic; in 1929 a Pennsylvania newspaper said that York County had no black cats because of a wave of witch-terror. The black cats were killed by throwing them into boiling water.
3. As late as the nineteenth century in Britain a woman was thrown into a pit simply because she had a black cat.
4. W. Carew Hazlitt, *Faiths & Folklore of the British Isles.*

twelve became witches. To prevent this from happening, people would cut a cross into the cat's skin. The superstition that cats could become witches and vice versa was so strong that people would never speak ill of anyone in front of a cat, for it might be a witch in disguise.

The hare was another animal form the witch could take.[5] The people of Britain often confused the hare, sacred animal of the Saxon goddess Eostre, and the cat because they were both associated with Moon goddesses. In Scotland, the Goddess of Witches was called Mither o' the Mawkins; however, the word *mawkin* or *malkin* meant either a hare or a cat.[6] Grimalkin (gray cat) became a favorite name for Pagan cats; gray malkins also meant the catkins on the pussy willow, whose blooming marks the Pagan rites in May.

The Christians went so far as to institute an annual ceremony on the Feast of St. John where they burned cats alive before the church doors. Black cats were especially sought for this ceremony because they were supposed to be extremely evil. This hideous practice soon spread to include the festivals of Midsummer, Easter, and Shrove Tuesday. To the Christians, the cat as minion of the devil could never suffer enough.[7]

A witch prepares herself with flying ointment, her cat familiar at her feet

---

5. Robert Briffault, *The Mothers*; James Frazer, *The Golden Bough*.
6. Potter & Sargent, *Pedigree*.
7. Frazer, *The Golden Bough*.

In the thirteenth century, Pope Gregory IX issued a statement that the Cathars (break-away Christians) bred black cats, the color of evil and sin,[8] which were of course the devil in disguise. Right after this declaration, the church declared a holy war against the Cathars, and any other persistent Pagan groups. The Knights Templar, a Christian order of knights created in the twelfth

century, was also accused of worshipping the devil in black cat form. Like the Cathars, the Templars were accused, tortured, killed, and their rich property confiscated by the church.

This was one of the first "official" statements by the church that branded the cat, and black cats in particular, as Lucifer's messengers. Anyone who associated with cats, especially black ones, was tarred with the same brush and called a witch and a servant of the devil.

The church appointed Inquisitors—all men—who had total authority over whom to convict, torture, murder, or set free. Extremely few of those accused of witchcraft were freed, as the

The "sport" of torturing cats is depicted in this detail from *The First Stage of Cruelty* by Hogarth

Inquisitor and all of those who helped him were paid through confiscation of the victim's property and belongings. Being an Inquisitor and a witch hunter became a very profitable business.

The Inquisitor Nicholas Remy pronounced judgment that all cats were really demons, and by 1387 it was widely "known" that witches worshipped the devil in the form of a cat.[9]

During the Renaissance, in 1489, Pope Innocent VIII sent out an official order to persecute all witches and kill all cats within Christian lands. Pope Innocent was also responsible for commissioning the *Malleus Maleficarum* (Ham-

---

8. All black animals were automatically condemned as minions of the devil. In fact, the witch today is still associated with the black cat. Barbara Walker, *The Woman's Dictionary of Symbols & Sacred Objects*.

9. Richard Cavendish, *The Powers of Evil*.

mer for Witches), the so-called "bible" of the witch hunters. This evil book was actually written by two German Dominican priests, Jakob Sprenger and Prior Heinrich Kramer. The church was not only responsible for beginning this terrible persecution against cats and those branded as witches, but many priests and good churchgoers actively took part in the tortures and murders, all with the blessings of the church.

For the next three centuries, the European churches hunted and persecuted witches and cats from Scandinavian countries to Spain and at last into the Americas.[10] This terrible practice continued until the seventeenth century, when Louis XIII ordered the persecution stopped in his country. However, at the coronation of Queen Elizabeth I in England, the Protestants filled a wickerwork dummy of the pope with live cats, carried it through the streets, and then threw it into a huge bonfire.

As late as the fifteenth century, the Norse cults of Freyja and Holda (Hel) still flourished against every threat of hell fire the church could invent. During this

This seventeenth-century edition of Olaus Magnus' *Historia Gentium Septentrionalibus* depicts witches raising a storm; the skull on the pole is probably that of a cat

10. In other countries outside the influence of the Christian church, cats were never persecuted and tortured. In the Eastern religions, for example, they taught the higher spiritual law of the unity of humans with all Nature and were more concerned with rewarding virtue than sitting in judgment.

time, Freyja was said to ride in a chariot pulled by twenty cats, while Holda was followed by a group of virgins disguised in cat skins. These Pagan groups met once a week, which probably cut into the once-a-week meetings of the church.

Soon, the church began its campaign against the Pagans who refused to join and support the churches. Church officials, who also saw great profit in Pagan lands, began to torture, hang, burn, and flay alive those whom they called witches, all in the excuse of saving souls. Drunk on their power, they did the same to cats. The law also condemned and punished in the same manner anyone who helped a sick or wounded cat, sheltered, or loved one.

During the infamous European witch hunts, witches and their cats were tried by a church court, automatically found guilty, tortured, and killed—usually by being burned alive. Although a few goats, toads, dogs, and other animals were said to be kept by witches, the most common accusation was against the cat.

Anyone who owns an ordinary black cat (distinct from a pedigreed Black Shorthair or Bombay) will notice that the cat usually has white on it somewhere. This white can be a tiny patch of a few white hairs or only a white whisker. The reason for this goes back to that most infamous period of European history: the witch hunts. During the burnings of millions of humans, the totally black cat suffered the same terrible fate, dying by the thousands. However, any cat who had the smallest touch of white was spared, as it was considered to be "redeemed" and not consecrated to the devil.[11] Because of this destruction, the completely black cat became very rare, while those with a touch of white survived.

Part of the reaction to the cat in general may have come from those who knew its ancient sacred heritage, especially in Egypt. Another reason may have been its connection with Pagan people, particularly the independent Pagan women. Added to this is the cat's uncanny ability to sense the true character of people and its refusal to become completely subservient to humans, like dogs. The church officials, playing on fear, said that the 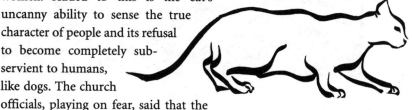 cat's nocturnal wanderings and its screeching during the breeding season were signs of secret orgies and ceremonies with the devil.[12]

---

11. Desmond Morris, *Catlore*.

12. For some reason, the Christian church has always been overly interested in sex, at the same time as they condemn it. Church officials of the time sweated their way through detailed sermons of sexual orgies by the devil and his cohorts and followers, while screaming against it. During the witch hunts, every condemned woman's body was obscenely viewed and handled, all in the name of saving her soul. All this was really a way for some man to get his sexual "kicks" while doing the "good" work of the church.

Because of the widespread destruction of cats during the witch hunt eras, cats were scarce when the Black Plague hit Europe. The fact of the matter is that the church and its paranoid ideas caused the death of millions of people, first through accusation of witchcraft, then through the plague, all because they had wantonly killed the very animal who could have killed the rats. At first the church encouraged the presence of rats in their dungeons. After all, they considered attack by packs of rats to be part of the legitimate torture of prisoners.

The first plague of black rats originated in Africa; they were stowaways in the ships of the first Crusaders returning from the Holy Land. Within fifty years, the rats had swarmed over all of Europe, spreading their deadly disease as they went. Fortunately, the Crusaders also brought back Palestinian cats, which helped control the rats. The cloisters, convents, and abbeys began to keep cats for protection against the rats.

Suddenly, the stronger, more prolific brown rat appeared in 1750. It quickly spread over Europe, from England to Spain and Egypt, and into the Americas by 1775. One of the first cases of plague recorded was in Napoleon's army in Egypt in 1799.[13] The rat population got so far ahead of the diminished cat population's ability to kill them that it is still a major threat today. The rat's lice and fleas still carry typhus, rat-bite fever, the plague, Weil's disease, and trichinosis.

By the late seventeenth century, when most people regained their senses and stopped torturing witches and cats, the persecution of cats began to wane. However, a new danger to black cats arose.

Pagan wise women and men, who had been the doctors, had been killed in the witch hunts or gone underground, and a new and very dangerous breed of physician evolved—men, and only men, sanctioned by the churches.

These early so-called doctors believed that cats caused a number of diseases in the most ludicrous ways. Sixteenth-century physician Ambroise Pare believed that through a cat's brain, hair, breath, and even its gaze, the cat could infect humans. According to Pare, even the cat's breath was poisonous. Even into the 1900s, the French doctor Matthiole said that if you slept with a cat you would get consumption and that cats carried leprosy.

These "doctors" also declared that certain vital parts of cats, and particularly black cats, were certain cures for a great variety of illnesses. They came up with some of the most horrid, ignorant medical remedies using black cats that the world has ever known. A fresh skin from a newly killed cat was supposed to cure rheumatism, sore throats, and hives. To avoid sickness, it was recommended that you cut off the

---

13. Napoleon absolutely hated cats and refused to let one anywhere near his army and camp.

tail of a black cat and bury it under your doorstep. For blindness, the head of a black cat was burned to ashes; then the ashes were blown into the eyes. Nine drops of blood from a cat's tail was mixed with nine roasted barley corns and the ointment applied to rashes.

There were also some hideous uses of cats during magickal rituals; these rituals were not performed by Pagans, but by Christians. One of these said to roast a live cat over a fire; its tormented screams would bring the King-cat,[14] who was compelled to answer any question you put to it. This hideous method of divination was called *taghgairm* by the Scottish Gaels. One can only speculate as to why Christians continued to practice this barbaric method of divination well into the 1700s.

Although the Arabs were admonished to respect cats and never chase them from tent or mosque, the mysterious brotherhood of Siddi Heddi engaged in a disgusting practice. They would entice ownerless cats into their sanctuaries, fatten them up and, at a ritual feast every year, kill and eat them. This was in direct violation of the Moslem law against eating any carnivorous animal.[15]

The ancient Egyptians were among the first cultures to believe that cats had the ability to see spirits. The ancient Britons said that if you stared deep into a cat's eyes, you would be able to see into the world of spirits. In the Gold Coast area of Africa, shamans wore cat skins around their necks; this was said to help them communicate with spirits.

It was not until the Victorian Era, in the 1800s, that cats once more became a popular household pet.

A girl plays with her pet cats in this vignette from the Victorian era

---

14. This King-cat was also called Big Ears.
15. Fernand Mery, *The Life, History & Magic of the Cat.*

Felines in Folklore, Literature, and Art

Cats have been portrayed in literature, sculpture, and paintings since very early times. Within the last two centuries the feline family has also appeared in movies, advertisements, comics, and on television. They may be shown as good or evil, depending upon the personal likes or dislikes of the creator of the product. However, cats are all around us and in a great variety of forms.

> A cat can be trusted to purr when she is pleased, which is more than can be said for human beings.
>
> —WILLIAM INGE

There are a great many folklore stories and fairy tales that feature cats. Most of them portray the cat as a wise, magickal creature who helps humans in some way. The rest represent the cat as a devious, dangerous animal who is not to be trusted and is more often than not in league with the devil.

The favorable cat tales come from times when the Goddess was still given respect, for the cat was one of Her sacred creatures. You can mark the invading influence of those who actively worked to destroy belief in the Goddess by the rise of negative stories about cats.

In Japan, cats are viewed in an ambivalent light. They are considered to be wise and powerful, yet at the same time not a creature to be trusted. The Buddhists tell a story of the cat and the death of Buddha. According to this tale, only the cat and the venomous serpent did not weep when Buddha died, the cat because he was more interested in hunting mice. An older Japanese superstition says that cats, like foxes and badgers, have the ability to bewitch humans.

Among Japanese sailors, the cat is highly regarded, especially the *mike-neko*, cat of three colors, which is greatly prized. The sailors say that a cat on a ship will keep off the spirits of those who have died in the oceans who might try to cause sailing disasters. In general, the cat is believed to have control over the spirits of any who have died.

Cats are featured in many folktales, such as this illustration depicting one variation of Puss in Boots

Among the fairy tales collected by the Brothers Grimm from the peasants of Hesse, Germany (published in two volumes, one in 1812 and the other in 1815), are several stories about cats. One such tale is the *Bremen Town Musicians*. Four old animals, a donkey, cat, dog, and rooster, ran away together to keep from being killed because of their age. The animals decided to go to the town of Bremen and become musicians. On the road, they took refuge in a house that they discovered was the hideout of robbers. When the robbers returned, the animals ran them off through some very smart thinking.

The moral of this story is that old animals can still be useful. By the same token, old humans can still be useful through their wisdom.

Another story is called the *Poor Miller's Apprentice and the Cat*. There was once an elderly miller who had three hired men, the youngest named Hans. The miller decided to retire and said he would give the mill to the apprentice who brought him the best horse. The apprentices started out together to search for the right horse, but the two older men sneaked off in the night and left the younger one sleeping in a deep cave. Hans soon met a little spotted cat, whom he helped by building a house and tending fields. In return, she promised to give him the finest horse ever if he would serve her for seven years.

At the end of seven years, the little cat told Hans to go back to the miller and promised to bring the horse to him. Hans had only his ragged old clothes to wear, but he was determined. When he reached the mill, the miller refused to let him sit at the table with the other apprentices because of his clothes. When night came, Hans had to sleep outside on hard straw.

On the third day, a coach drawn by six magnificent horses came to the inn and out stepped a beautiful princess, who was really the little cat. She gave the promised horse to the miller, who agreed that Hans should now have the mill. The princess told the miller to keep the mill, for Hans had better things awaiting him.

The third story of the Brothers Grimm is probably the best known—*Puss in Boots*. When a certain miller died, the two older sons took the mill and the

Dore's classic depiction of a strapping Puss in Boots

donkey, leaving the youngest son with only a cat. When they were alone, the cat began to talk. He asked the boy to make him a pair of boots so he could go out among people and help the boy. The boy made the boots, and the cat put them on.

The cat became friends with a nearby king by bringing him partridges, saying they were a gift from his lord the Count. In return, the king gave the cat all the gold he could carry. The cat immediately took the gold back to the boy. This went on for some time, until the cat managed to get the king and princess and Hans together.

To help Hans in his role as Count, the cat tricked a nearby sorcerer into turning himself into a mouse, which the cat immediately ate. Thus, Hans got a magnificent castle. The miller boy and the princess were married. When the king died, the Count became king and Puss in Boots was his prime minister.

The Brothers Grimm also tell another story of the cat who accidentally lost the dog's certificate of nobility and thus forfeited their friendship forever. This story appears to be an attempt to explain the animosity between cats and dogs.

In the fables of the Greek writer Aesop the cat is always portrayed as a trickster, one who couldn't be trusted and who could outwit even the fox.

The Greeks also had a little-known story that tells of the Sun and the Moon creating all the animals at the beginning of the world. The Sun created the lion; not to be outdone, the Moon created the cat, who is infinitely more useful to humans.

Throughout France, there are several tales and a deep belief in what are called matagots, or magician cats. These special black cats can serve nine

The animosity between cats and dogs has been portrayed in literature and art for centuries

masters and make all of them very wealthy. Since one can never be certain which black cat is a matagot, all black cats are loved and fed well.

In the British story, Dick Whittington's famous cat was considered to be a *matagot*. Although the form of this story that we know was first published in Andrew Lang's *The Blue Fairy Book* in 1889, it existed in Europe as far back as the thirteenth century.

The same legend of the cat who makes his master wealthy is found in the folklore of Denmark, Persia, and Italy at least a century before the story of Dick Whittington of London.

In his book *Just So Stories*, Rudyard Kip—ling wrote a cat story called *The Cat Who Walked By Himself*, still a favorite with children. This tale takes place in the very beginning of human civilization when, of all the wild animals in the Wet Wild Woods, the cat was the wildest of all. He walked by himself, and all places were alike to him. Through cunning, the cat tricked Woman, who lived in a cave, into letting him have a permanent place by the fire and all he could eat, without being a servant. At first the cat entertained the baby and kept him from crying. When a mouse ran across the floor and the cat caught it, his place by the fire was ensured.

Although the cat now lives with humans, when the Moon is high at night, he still walks by himself, waving his wild tail, and all places are alike to him.

In one telling of the story of Noah's ark,[1] the devil got inside the ark without Noah knowing about it. He turned himself into a mouse and began to gnaw a hole in the bottom of the boat. Unable to catch the mouse or stop the damage to the boat, Noah asked the lion for help. The lion sneezed, and a pair of cats came from its nostrils.[2] Immediately, the cats jumped on the devil-mouse and ate it.

---

1. Stith Thompson, *The Folktale*.
2. Carol Ochs, *Behind the Sex of God*.

The children's nursery rhyme "Hey diddle diddle, the cat and the fiddle" has an underlying sacred theme, found also in ancient traditions of Rome, Gaul, and the Celtic cultures. The original theme appears to be ancient Egyptian.[3] The cat would be the cat-headed goddess Bast; the dog, the jackal-headed Anubis; and the cow, the sky and lunar goddess Nut. The fiddle represents the sistrum of Isis, while the spoon and dish symbolize ritual vessels.

Celtic tradition, not knowing the domesticated cat until it was introduced by Mediterranean traders, looked on the cat as a creature with chthonic powers. Irish legend mentions a Little Cat who guarded a treasure; any thief who tried to steal the treasure was burned to ashes when Little Cat turned into pure flame.

A legend from Connaught at Clogh-magh-right-cat (now Clough) tells of a Slender Black Cat who lived in a cave-shrine there before the coming of Christianity.[4] This Cat reclined on a chair of old silver and gave oracular answers to those who sought her. Like the Delphic Oracle, the Irish Cat gave scornful answers to those who tried to deceive her.

Robert Graves wrote that a cat cult once existed in Ireland and appeared to center on the Knowth burial chamber.[5] In the old writings called *The Proceedings of the Grand Bardic Academy*, we find the tale of the great King-cat of Ireland. The King-cat, whose name was Irusan, was said to have lived in the Knowth burial chamber in County Meath at one time in the far past. The King-cat was described as being as large as a plow ox. When the chief ollave of Ireland, Seanchan Torpest, satirized this King-cat, the creature got his revenge by putting the ollave on his back and carrying him far away.

There is also an old Irish tale of a mysterious island inhabited by men with cat heads. This is probably a reference to a clan of Irish people who considered the cat to be their totem animal and wore helmets shaped like cats' heads.

The folk tale *Cinderella* comes from a much older story, of which there are several cultural versions, one of which is an Italian version called *Cinders-Cat*. There was once a kind-hearted, beautiful girl who was mistreated by her family and forced to wear a cat skin as clothing. She was called Cinders-Cat and had to

3. J. C. Cooper, *Symbolic & Mythological Animals.*
4. This is a very interesting description of an Irish cat as the only cat known was the European wild cat, which is not totally black in color and is of a stocky build. This description of the Slender Black Cat is identical to the Egyptian sacred cats in the temples of Bast and Pasht.
5. Robert Graves, *The White Goddess*, says that this cat-cult existed at about the same time as New Grange.

sleep on the hearth. Finally, her true beauty was discovered by a handsome, wealthy man who married her.

In the English version, called *Catskin*, the unwanted girl also had to wear a cat skin, sleep by the hearth, and do all the dirty servant-work. When the king gave a ball, the girl secretly went. A handsome nobleman fell in love with her and married her.

The Danes also had a version of this story. The kindhearted but mistreated girl was thrashed for giving milk to hungry, stray cats. In spite of this, she fed the next poor cat to come to the door. After drinking the milk, the cat grew very large and pushed off its skin, which it gave to the girl to use as a cloak. Later, the cat returned with beautiful dresses for the girl. Finally, through the girl's kindness, the cat was able to change into human shape; he was the enchanted brother of the king. The young man and the girl were married.

Even the Irish had a similar story, but instead of the mistreated girl being connected with the cat, it was the fairy godmother who was a cat.

The Norse have two myths in which cats are mentioned. When the wolf Fenris had to be bound, the gods found themselves in trouble after the great wolf easily broke the first two chains they used. Freyr's servant Skirnir was sent to the dwarfs in Svartalfheim for a magickal chain that could not be broken. These dwarfs made an extremely light, soft fetter, smooth and pliable as a silk ribbon, called *Gleipnir*. They forged this indestructible fetter out of the beard of a woman, the roots of the mountains, the breath of a fish, the spittle of a bird, and the sound of a cat walking.[6]

Another time the god Thorr journeyed to Utgard, home of the Frost Giants. Accompanied by the trickster Loki, he finally came to an ice castle, home of the king Utgard-Loki. Thorr received a rather cool welcome from the Giants, as he was always fighting them. Finally, Thorr was challenged by Utgard-Loki to prove his strength. A huge gray cat leaped forward, and Utgard-Loki challenged the thunder god to lift it off the ground. Although the strongest of all the gods ever born, Thorr was only able to lift one of the cat's paws. The Giants ridiculed Thorr for being a puny weakling. Later, Utgard-Loki admitted that the cat was really the great Midgard Serpent, called Jormungand.

Jormungand was one of the offspring of Loki and Angrboda, a Giantess, and was said to be so strong and huge that it encircled the world with its body. Cats have long been connected with snakes because of their hissing.

---

6. Rudolf Simek, *Dictionary of Northern Mythology.* Kevin Crossley-Holland, *The Norse Myths.*

There is a very old Italian legend that a cat gave birth to a litter of kittens in the stable where Mary birthed her son.

Another Italian fairy tale tells about a woman who had a lot of children and very little money. One day a fairy came to the woman and told her that if she climbed a certain high mountain she would find a palace inhabited only by cats; these cats would give alms to needy people. So the woman climbed up to the palace and was met at the door by a kitten. The woman offered to help the cats in any way she could and at once set about cooking, cleaning, and making them all comfortable. Finally, she went before the King of the Cats and asked him for alms. The King questioned the other cats and found that the woman had willingly done a lot of work, so he ordered that the cats fill her apron with gold coins.

A much older Roman myth tells the story of the goddess Diana who shapeshifted into a cat to escape from the evil Typhon. Hyginus, in his *Poetic Astronomy*, wrote that Typhon suddenly appeared in Greece and attacked not only the land and people, but the gods themselves. The gods changed themselves into animals and fled: Mercury as an ibis, Apollo as a crane, and Diana as a cat.

Ovid records a Greek myth about the loyal servant of Princess Alcemene, who gave birth to Heracles, son of Zeus. When Alcemene was ready to give birth to her son, jealous Hera did everything she could to prevent the birth. The servant Galinthias played a trick on Hera, which drew the goddess' attention and allowed Alcemene to give birth. Hera was so angry she turned Galinthias into a cat and banished her to the Underworld. Galinthias became a priestess of Hecate, queen of witches.

In the folk tales of eastern Europe is a story of a lazy wife who blamed the disorder of her house and the population of destructive mice on the old cat. The husband decided to beat the cat and ordered the lazy wife to hold the animal. Although he managed to land just two blows on the cat, the wife was terribly scratched—a just punishment for her lies.

In cat stories from Russia, the cats are always very large, generous, and full of good will and cunning. Ivanovitch was a cat who used his cunning to marry a fox and thus become king over all the forest animals. The unnamed tabby tom who lived with the goddess Baba Yaga took pity on a tender-hearted girl and substituted himself in order to save the girl's life.

Another Russian legend says that, in the beginning, a cat and a dog were given the task of guarding the gates of Paradise. The devil disguised himself as a mouse and tried to creep by them. The dog ignored this pseudo-mouse and let him pass, but the cat pounced on him and threw him out again.

One of the legends about the pussy willow comes from Poland. A mother cat had a litter of kittens that her owners didn't want, so the humans threw the baby cats into the river to drown. The mother paced the bank, crying for her little ones. The willows growing along the banks of the river were touched by the mother cat's grief and trailed their branches in the water. The kittens caught the branches in their paws and climbed to safety. Now each spring the willow has little velvet buds, symbolic of the kittens they saved.

There is a Scandinavian cat tale that is also found among the folk tales in India. Once there was a strange, magickal, but greedy cat who waited until her mistress was gone from the cottage and then ate all the porridge, the bowl that held the porridge, and the ladle. When the mistress returned and commented on what a fat cat she was, the cat ate the mistress. Still hungry, the cat went out and ate a great many other animals until she burst.

A story from the 1800s tells of a fisherman who became very poor because he was sick. A cat, whom the fisherman had fed every day when the man had visited his owner, changed himself into the shape of a man so he could give the old man two gold coins. This was the cat's way of thanking the man for being kind to him.

In the Far East there are hundreds of stories about cats taking the shape of old women, priests, courtesans, and young girls so that they can deceive their victims. In this area of the world, it is also thought that the cat gains the power of speech at a certain advanced age.

There are many Japanese paintings that show a pair of running cats. These designs are based on the story of two star-crossed lovers who were forbidden to see each other. In order to be together, they magically transformed themselves into cats and ran away.

In India the cat is considered to be a very magickal creature and a bringer of luck. One of their legends tells the tale of Patripatan, a cat so cunning and insidious that he climbed into the realm of the gods to plead for his master, the prince of the kingdom of Salangham. In Devendiren, a sky land, twenty-four million gods and forty-eight million goddesses reigned, and

Patripatan enchanted them all. He especially became a favorite of the king of the gods and the most beautiful of the goddesses. Although the cat didn't return for three hundred years, his master the prince and all the people of that kingdom didn't age at all. When Patripatan did return, he carried in his white paws a flowering branch of the holy Parasidam.

There are also many tales of cats in the Americas. In Native American legends, Wild Cat is portrayed as the younger brother of Coyote and represents stealth. The Tiger Cat, or Cat-a-Mountain, is said to be noted for his fierceness and ingratitude. In the hunting rituals of the Zuni, the Wild Cat replaces Badger.

Ccoa, a Peruvian legendary cat, was considered to be a storm spirit; he had a huge head, with hail falling from his eyes and ears. Another South American cat-monster was Guirivulu, whose tail ended in a sharp claw; he could change himself into a giant snake and live in the water.

The feline family is not part of the native animals of Australia, but the Aboriginal tribes have a totem animal known as Wild Cat.

Cats have been immortalized in more recent literature, as well as in the folk tale,[7] and have been the favorite pet companion of many writers. All three of the Bronte sisters loved cats, as did Victor Hugo, Ernest Hemingway, Colette, Charles Dickens, Mark Twain, and H. G. Wells.

T. S. Eliot wrote a poem called *The Naming of Cats*. In this poem, he tells how each cat has three names: the formal name, the family name, and a secret name known only to the cat. He also wrote *Old Possum's Book of Practical Cats* in 1939; the award-winning musical *Cats* is based on this story.

The names we humans bestow on our cats are varied and unique. I have known cats named Purry Como, Eartha Cat, Butch and Sundance (two terrors as kittens), Tuxedo (for his white shirt-front), Purrl Bailey, Muff (a white longhaired Persian), Misha (a part Siamese with an Oriental air of dignity; his name is a diminutive of the Russian name Mikhail), Zorri, Beowulf and Valkyrie (two warrior kittens), Flash (he survived dogs as a kitten because he ran so fast), Finnigan (the six-toed Irish fighter), Fox and Sox (a red kitten and one with white feet), Midnight (coal black), and Chatter (a non-stop talking Siamese).

The feline family, especially domesticated cats, have been featured in innumerable paintings, including the art of the postage stamp. For some reason, the U.S. has never seen fit to grace its stamps with a portrait of the cat. Other countries, however, have some beautiful cat stamps, about one hundred of them, in fact. In 1930 Spain issued a stamp that shows Charles Lindbergh in the upper

---

7. Examples can be found in *The Literary Cat*, edited by Jean-Claude Suares and Seymour Chwast.

left corner and a black cat in the lower right near the Spirit of St. Louis; the cat belonged to Lindy, who left it behind rather than risk its life. Luxembourg issued a stamp in 1966 that represented the witch's cat of the Middle Ages. In 1967 Turkey put out a stamp with a white Angora. The following year a Polish stamp honored Puss in Boots of folklore.

Cats have also garnered their share of parts in movies, TV, and cartoons. Who could forget Pyewacket in the movie *Bell, Book & Candle* or Leo, the famous MGM lion? Or the cartoon smart-cat Garfield? But did you know that the first cat to be featured in a cartoon was Mr. Jack in 1899? Mr. Jack, an orange and black striped tiger in men's clothes, was popular for more than forty years.

Cats are featured on everything from stamps to bookplates, such as this bookplate from 1900

The early 1900s saw several cats portrayed in newspaper comic strips. The first domestic cat to appear in cartoons was Krazy Kat, who appeared in 1910 in a comic strip called "The Dingbat Family." For more than thirty years, Krazy Kat was enjoyed by readers, including President Woodrow Wilson and the poet E. E. Cummings. In 1914, the cat Kitty appeared in "Polly and Her Pals." This feline was followed by Felix in an animated silent cartoon in 1919; Felix was also the star of the first "talkie" cartoon, one year before Mickey Mouse came on the scene. By 1923 Felix was put into the newspapers.

During the hard times of the 1930s the cartoon "Archie and Mehitabel" appeared; this revolved around the friendship between an alley cat and a cockroach. "Cicero's Cat" and "Spooky" came next. The 1934 cat comic "The Pussycat Princess" was created by the woman who created the chubby-cheeked Campbell Soup Kids.

The Hanna-Barbera duo Tom and Jerry became popular in the 1940s and 1950s, but the role of the cat had changed. Most modern comic depictions of cats casts these creatures into a negative role. The 1945 debut of Sylvester shows us a cat who isn't too bright and who is always defeated by a little bird. In Walt Disney's *Cinderella* (1950) the cat Lucifer is cast as an absolute villain, merely for hunting mice. By 1955 Disney came out with *Lady and the Tramp*, which again had two villainous cats, this time Siamese. *Alice in Wonderland* has the Cheshire cat, while *Gay Purree* (featuring the voice of Judy Garland as

Mewsette, Robert Goulet as Jaune Tom, and Hermione Gingold as Madame Rubens-Chatte) appeared in 1962. L. Frank Baum, who wrote the *Wizard of Oz* (which had the Cowardly Lion), also featured cats in his books. And who can forget Dr. Seuss' *Cat in the Hat?* The 1960s cartoon of "Top Cat" shows Top and his "gang" in New York City, always in trouble with Officer Dibble.

However, there have been a few modern positive roles for cats in Disney films, such as Figaro in *Pinocchio* (1940), *The Nine Lives of Thomasina* (where a cat meets the goddess Bast), the group of cats in *The Aristocats* (1970), and Rufus in *The Rescuers* (1977). Other modern and positive cat comics are "Garfield" (1978), "Kit 'N' Carlyle" (1980), "Calvin and Hobbes" (1985), and "Eek the Cat" on the Fox Network.

Cats have also appeared in books by Robert Heinlein and Joy Adamson (*Born Free*). They have had parts in such television series as *Star Trek* and *Mission Impossible.*

Tom and Jerry

Lucifer, the spoiled housecat belonging to Cinderella's wicked stepmother

Scat Cat's Swingin' Band, from *The Aristocats*

Cats have hobnobbed with some of Hollywood's elite over the years. The film industry also used cats in several movies besides *Bell, Book & Candle* (starring James Stewart and Kim Novak). The James Mason movie *I Met a Murderer* had felines in scenes, as did his films *The Upturned Glass* and *The Seventh Veil*. Ethel Barrymore's cat appeared with her in *Night Song*. Other movie stars, such as Errol Flynn, Mary Martin, Natalie Wood, and Olivia de Haviland all had special friendships with cats.

©Archive Photos

Kim Novak and Pyewacket from the 1958 movie *Bell, Book & Candle*

A great many writers have also shared their lives with cats. Disney's movie *That Darn Cat* was made from the book *Undercover Cat*, which featured Pancho Gordon, the black feline belonging to the mystery writers Gordon and Mildred Gordon. The French writer Colette put her ginger cat Prrou in her novel *Retreat From Love*, green-eyed Peronnella in *Chance Acquaintances*, Saha in *The Cat*, and La Chatte in *Break of Day*. Many of Mark Twain's works mention cats, among them *Letters From the Earth; The Innocents Abroad; Roughing It*; and of course *Tom Sawyer*. Twain kept nineteen cats at his Connecticut house.

Cats have also been used to promote products. Everyone is familiar with Morris and the cat food commercials. However, the cat as salesperson goes back much further than Morris.

Black Cat cigarettes were sold in the late 1800s. Starry Gold, a French manufacturer of fountain pens, used a white cat to market its ware. I have a Tiger Tobacco tin, made in the early 1900s, which is about the size of a lunch box. In the early 1900s, a German firm made a white wine called Zeller Schwarze Katz (Black Cat wine), so named because of the black cat pictured on the barrel. In the 1930s and 40s, the Eveready battery company used pictures of cats to symbolize their product's durability, obviously based on the cat's nine lives. Cats have been used to promote underwear, stove polish, cigars, sewing thread, and a variety of other products. During World War I and II, cats were even pictured on wartime recruiting posters.

Whatever our personal feelings toward the tribe of tiger, we seem to be unable or unwilling to live in a world that has no representations of cats.

Cat-Vampires and Demon Cats

Even though many cultures revered and loved the cat, there are also many horror tales of demon-cats who either terrified humankind because of their evilness or used their feline abilities to exact punishment for terrible deeds done to their own kind.

Cats are smarter than dogs. You can't get eight cats to pull a sled through snow.

—JEFF VALDEZ

There have been some weird experiences with the figures of Egyptian mummified cats or their sarcophagi. More than one owner of such an item had terrifying dreams, heard strange noises, and saw horrible apparitions. Several men died of fright or killed themselves after finding or purchasing such artifacts.

One amateur archaeologist put an unopened cat sarcophagus in his study so he could admire it every day. Late one night, as he sat reading, he heard a sharp crack and looked up to find the sarcophagus neatly opened along the sealed seams. As he watched, a thin cloud of black dust arose as the cat mummy disintegrated before his eyes. That night he suffered the first of a long series of terrifying nightmares. Even during the day he was nervous about dim corners and dark hallways, for he said that he saw burning eyes watching him all the time. Within a year, he died of a sudden heart attack.

The remaining cat sarcophagus was inherited by his son, who soon discovered he had inherited the irate cat spirit as well. The eyes began haunting the son day and night until he began to fear he would commit suicide. Finally, he sold it to a collector, who also died mysteriously within a year. After that, the haunted cat sarcophagus and its avenging spirit disappeared from sight, never to be heard of again.

The Japanese both liked and distrusted the cat. Although they treated their cats with great respect, they still had tales of vampire cats who, like the fox and badger, were capable of shapeshifting, tricking, and bewildering humans.

When it comes to Japanese tales of vampires, the vampire is often a cat who takes on the form of its victim afterward. Perhaps this idea comes from the Chinese belief that if a corpse laid out on a bed has a dog under the bed and a cat on the roof above, the dead person will become a vampire. A similar belief is found in some parts of Europe, where it is said that if a cat walks over a corpse it will be turned into a vampire.

The most famous Japanese cat-vampire tale (*The Cat of Nabeshima*) concerns the Prince of Hizen and his favorite lady, O Toyo. One night at midnight a huge double-tailed cat[1] appeared in O Toyo's chambers. Before she could scream, this demon-cat sprang at her throat and killed her. The cat dug a hole under the veranda, buried the woman, and took on her shape. The prince saw no difference in his beloved, but each day after she visited him, he got weaker and weaker. The cat demon was slowly draining his blood. The doctors were puzzled and prescribed all kinds of medicine, but nothing helped.

The prince noticed that he always grew weaker at night, so he ordered a hundred servants to stand guard around his bed while he slept. The cat demon, in woman form, cast a spell causing the servants to sleep while she continued to drain the life from the prince.

Desperate, the prince's councilors begged a priest to pray for their prince. While at prayer, this priest was disturbed by a young soldier, whose name was Ito Soda. The soldier asked to be allowed to stand guard; his request was granted.

---

1. Japanese cat-demons are all said to have forked or double tails, which gives them doubly strong powers of enchantment. Half a world away in Ireland, there are also legends of cats with two or nine tails. Originally, the cat-o'-nine-tails was a symbol of power and royalty.

At ten o'clock, as before, the other guards fell asleep, but Ito Soda stuck his dagger into his thigh to keep awake. When the cat-woman entered the room, she couldn't cast her spells over the prince because Ito Soda wouldn't let her get near. After two nights, the prince began to get better. Ito Soda, knowing that the beautiful O Toyo was now really an evil demon, went to her quarters and tried to kill her. Unable to defeat the young soldier, the cat demon changed back into its true form and fled into the mountains. After the prince fully regained his strength, he organized a hunt for the cat demon and destroyed it.

A witch turns into a cat in this nineteenth-century Japanese woodcut by Kuniyoshi

Another story tells of a Japanese knight who, along with a dog, killed a female jinn who demanded human sacrifices. As the knight was journeying into the mountains, he spent a night at a ruined temple. At midnight he awoke to see ghostly cats dancing and chanting, "Don't tell Shippeitaro." Then they disappeared. The next day, the knight came to a village and found the people very upset because they had to take their most beautiful girl to the jinn.

The knight remembered what he had seen and heard in the temple, and asked who Shippeitaro was. The villagers said it was the name of a brave dog who belonged to a nearby prince. The knight went to the prince, explained the situation, and returned with the dog. He put the dog in a cage and dragged it to the jinn's temple, where he waited until midnight. The phantom cats appeared with their leader, an enormous tomcat who screamed in delight at the sight of the cage. Suddenly, the knight threw open the cage door and Shippeitaro grabbed the giant cat in his teeth. The knight killed it with his sword. Then the dog chased away all the phantom cats, and the village was free.

There is an account from 1708 C.E. about a samurai and some very strange happenings in his house.[2] Glowing balls of light, which no one could catch, bounced through the rooms, once even illuminating a tree in the courtyard.

---

2. This is found in a scroll called the *Yamato Kwai-I ki*.

The women servants began to be attacked by spirits while they slept. One young woman was particularly singled out; her spinning wheel turned by itself and her pillow would revolve like a top when she lay down. The samurai called upon sorceresses, Shinto priests, and Buddhist priests to rid his house of the demon spirits, but nothing worked.

Finally, one night when the spirits were especially active, the samurai went into the courtyard and happened to look up at the roof. A strange and sinister sight met his eyes. A very old cat was walking on its hind legs on the roof. Around its head was wrapped a towel belonging to the young woman servant. The samurai motioned to one of his guards, who shot the cat with an arrow. The hauntings in the house stopped immediately and never returned. This demon-cat was huge and had a split tail (called *nekomata* by the Japanese).

Another Japanese myth says that cats were created to hunt and kill the rats who bit off the devil's tongue.

Ancient legends from Japan also include a tale of a Japanese bogeyman, a human whose name was Neko-Bake. This man was a sorcerer and a cannibal. In order to enter houses at night, Neko-Bake would take the shape of a cat. He was said to steal disobedient children and eat them.

The Chinese saw the cat as a shapeshifter, a nocturnal animal they classified as yin and associated with the powers of evil.

One early Chinese legend is the story of a cat owned by an emperor. After it had rained for three days, the cat went outside to bathe in a pool of water. Instantly, the cat was transformed into a dragon and flew away, never to be seen again.

In sixth-century China, they strongly believed in what they called cat-specters. When these cat-specters served a human, they could be sent to kill someone and then draw the dead person's possessions to the person who sent them.

A story dated 595 c.e. tells of a young man named T'o, whose wife had a servant who served a cat-specter. T'o wanted money for alcohol and convinced his wife to send the cat-specter to the empress to bewitch her so she would bestow gifts on T'o. The empress became very ill but the physicians didn't know what caused the illness. The emperor, however, was advised by his wise men that the empress was under the spell of a cat-specter. The only way to destroy this spirit was to kill the person who sent it.

In a short time, T'o's female slave was again sent to the palace. But this time she was met by the emperor's guards and told to recall the cat-specter at once or lose her life. The woman set out a bowl of rice gruel and drummed on the bowl with a spoon. When the cat-specter arrived, the woman became blue in the face and staggered about. Certain now of the culprit, the emperor was issuing orders for T'o and his wife to commit suicide, when T'o's brother begged for the emperor's mercy. T'o lost all his possessions and position; his wife was sent to become a Buddhist nun. The emperor immediately sought out all those who kept cat-specters and exiled them to remote parts of China.

It was a common Chinese belief of this era that people sometimes changed into cats at death in order to get revenge on enemies. One empress sentenced a court lady to death. "Fine," replied the lady. "When I die, I will take on a cat form and come back and change you into a rat. Then I will kill you." The empress changed her mind. The Asians have a saying that if you are afraid of or dislike cats, you must have been a rat in your last incarnation.

The Chinese also have a legend about tigers being able to recall souls after death. The tiger is supposed to have a certain hair in its tail that has the power to bring back the soul to a dead body, very similar to the soul being returned to the body when a vampire is made.

Celtic cultures rarely had friendly or helpful cats in their legends. The Celtic felines were described as Monster Cats instead. Perhaps this is because the only

cat they knew was the untamable, fierce European wild cat.

In Welsh tales, the enchanted sow Henwen had originally been a human; actually, Henwen portrays an aspect of the goddess Cerridwen.[3] Henwen, big with young, was tended by her keeper, a young man whose name was Coll. Because there was a prophecy that Henwen's offspring would harm Britain, King Arthur set out to destroy her. He chased the sow down to Land's End in Cornwall, but she swam out to sea with Coll hanging on to her bristles.

At each place the sow landed, she gave birth to three grains of wheat, one of barley, one of rye, three bees, a pig, a wolf cub, and an eagle. At last, Henwen landed with Coll at Arvon. There, under a black stone, she gave birth to a kitten. Coll immediately threw the kitten into the Menai Straits, where the sons of Paluc (from the Isle of Man) rescued it. It grew up to be the ferocious Paluc (sometimes called Palug) Cat, one of the Three Plagues of Anglesey, the Great

---

3. The Welsh goddess Cerridwen, an aspect of the Crone, had a fierce, unpleasant side.

Cat who could eat nine score warriors at one time. Sir James Frazer links the Palug Cat with the monster Chapalu of French Arthurian legend.

The Scottish Highlands are full of tales of elfin or fairy cats, known as the Cait Sith [cait shee]. These are said to be black cats, as big as a large dog, with arched backs, erect hair, and white spots on their chests. However, the Gaels of the Highlands believed that the Cait Sith was a witch transformed into a cat, not a fairy. Another demonic cat who was even larger and more fierce was Big Ears, who only appeared when cats were roasted to death.

The cats on the Isle of Man are said to have their own king. By day, this king appears to be an ordinary cat, but at night he has terrible powers. If anyone mistreats him or his subject cats, the king will seek the person out at night and take a horrible revenge.

This French legend, found in the fourteenth-century manuscript called *Le Roman de Merlin*,[4] begins with a man finding a black kitten caught in his fishing net. He took it home and fed it. Soon the cat was so huge that it strangled the fisherman and his family, then fled to the mountains where it terrorized the countryside.

King Arthur, with Merlin and his knights, set out to conquer this demon-cat. Through Merlin's powers, they found its lair in a deep cave in the mountainside. The sorcerer whistled to get the cat out of the cave. It made one great leap at Arthur, breaking his spear into pieces. Arthur knocked the cat demon to the ground with his shield, but its claws penetrated his armor and drew blood. Arthur attacked the cat again, but this time the creature sank its claws into his shield and wouldn't let go. Arthur cut off the fore legs, but the great cat gripped him with its hind feet and bit his chest and shoulders until he was covered with his own blood. To win the battle, Arthur had to hack the great cat demon into pieces. Tradition says that Arthur disappeared after this battle, dying of the wounds inflicted by the cat.

An Irish story of a demon-cat is given in the works of William Butler Yeats and Lady Gregory,[5] originally published in 1888. Once there was a very lucky fisherman in Connemara. The man's wife always had plenty of fish to sell, but a great cat came every night and ate the best fish. The woman was determined to catch this cat. While the wife and the younger woman sat spinning, the door flew open and in walked a big black cat. The creature made itself comfortable by the fire and growled at the women.

---

4. Patricia Dale-Green, *Cult of the Cat*.
5. *A Treasury of Irish Myth & Folklore*. This same story is told in *Folk Tales of the British Isles*, edited by Kevin Crossley-Holland.

The younger woman jumped up and called the cat the devil. At this, the cat scratched deep gouges in her arm and warned her not to call him names. Then he barred the door and held the women prisoner. When the fisherman came and attacked the cat with a stick, the cat scratched his face and drove him away.

Spying the fish on the table, the cat selected the biggest and best and began to eat them. The wife hit it with a pair of tongs, but the cat only grinned at her. Then both women attacked it with sticks. The cat spat fire and scratched them until the blood ran down their faces and arms.

Finally, the wife got out a bottle of holy water and threw it over the cat. With an unearthly scream, the black cat dissolved into a thick cloud of black smoke with two fiery red eyes. When the smoke cleared, the only thing that remained was a shriveled body, and even that soon disappeared.

The Irish hero Cu Chulainn was attacked one night by three supernatural cats who only disappeared at dawn. Cu Chulainn hit one of the cats on the head with his sword but the blade rang as if it struck stone.

A legend about St. Brendan, a Celtic holy man, tells of a great sea cat. Brendan and his monks went in search of the Land of Promise and ran into a storm, which forced them to land on a rocky island. As they came ashore, an old man called out a warning to flee because of a huge, dangerous sea cat who lived there. The old man said the cat had come to the island with him as an ordinary kitten, but as soon as the cat began to eat the strange fish that washed up on the shore, it began to grow and change. It became huge and very ferocious, attacking anything that came near it.

As the old man told his story, Brendan and his monks heard a terrible yowl rise above the winds of the storm. They didn't wait to see what it was, but jumped back into their boat and rowed away as fast as they could, leaving the old man alone on the shore.

When they were some distance from the island, they looked back. An animal the size of a small pony ran across the sands and leaped into the water. It was the demon monster cat. With powerful strokes, the cat easily paddled toward them, its great eyes shining "like vessels of glass" through the storm.

Frightened, the monks began to pray. Just as the monster cat reached a paw up to climb into the boat, a second cat just as big swam close and attacked it. The great cats screamed and hissed and fought in the roiling water while Brendan and his monks rowed swiftly away.

In the *Kalevala* of Finland, a collection of ancient Finnish tales, there is a story of a sorcerer who went into a house full of men and enchanted them. Then he threw the men onto a sledge, which was pulled by a huge cat. This cat swiftly took the men to the far-off limits of Pohjola, the Underworld, a place of darkness and evil spirits.

Spanish Hebrew folklore has a story blaming vampirism on Lilith, Adam's first wife. Lilith was driven out of the Garden of Eden because she refused to obey all of Adam's wishes. She changed herself into an evil witch and a vampire to get her revenge on the descendants of Adam. In her favorite disguise of a huge black cat, named El Broosha, Lilith was said to go about at night, sucking the blood of newborn babies.

The demon-cat, the cat serpent (Jormungand), the sea cat seen by St. Brendan, the Chinese cat dragon, the Celtic Paluc cat, and all the other forms of dark felines symbolize the Underworld and the power of death over life.

Eastern Europe has always had more tales of vampires and vampire-animals than any other area. Many people in this region still believe that if a cat walks or jumps across a corpse, any innocent dead person will become a vampire.[6] This idea comes from the belief that the cat carries the "seed" or "germ" of vampirism, making it a potential vampire who can infect other creatures.

A story of cat-transferred vampirism was recorded in the seventeenth century in an area called Silesia. An older man died after he was kicked by his horse. As he drew his last breath, a black cat jumped onto the bed and violently scratched his face. After the funeral, the ghost of this man was seen by several people. Soon stories of bowls of milk being turned into blood, old men strangled, babies stolen, and chickens killed began to circulate through the town.

For six months, the strange incidences continued, until at last the villagers decided to dig up the dead man whom they believed to be the cause of their troubles. They found his body fresh and flexible, the eyes able to open and close. When they cut a vein in one leg, it bled freely. They hacked up the body and burned it. After that, the troubles ceased.

---

6. The same belief exists in many Celtic countries as well.

During the Salem witch trials in the U.S., a story of a demon-cat called Tail-rings began to circulate. One of the accused women was named Strmantis, who foresaw her death at the hands of the Puritan torturers. Before they caught her, Strmantis killed a ring-tailed cat and stuffed its skin with straw mixed with certain magickal herbs. She substituted moonstones for its eyes and extremely sharp blades for its claws. Then she performed a ritual that would bring the cat to life whenever she spoke the final words of the spell, which she planned to do when the witch hunters came for her.

It wasn't long before the Puritan witch hunters broke into Strmantis' house. As they grabbed her, she screamed out the final words, and Tailrings got away through a window. It didn't take her captors long to condemn and murder Strmantis. However, their troubles had just begun with Tailrings.

The cat began to exact retribution for the murder of its mistress and filled Salem and the surrounding countryside with fear. Hunters would see the glowing moonstone eyes as Tailrings watched them in the dark woods. The cat stalked, attacked, and slashed up one person after another. No hunter was ever able to hit Tailrings with an ordinary musket ball. After many years, the attacks by Tailrings grew fewer, until finally the cat was seen no more. Perhaps all the people responsible for the torture and murder of accused witches were dead by that time, and there was no further reason for Tailrings to exist.

The tales of demon and vampire cats, cats who haunt and persecute humans, and those cats who exact revenge for misdeeds against their kind may have originated from the ancient belief of the cat being associated with specific deities. Many of the gods and goddesses who were connected with the feline family often had darker sides to their nature. They were the impartial judges of human deeds and intentions; it was their duty to see that the scales of spiritual justice were balanced. The cat, or other feline member, was their instrument by which they exacted the justice due. A deep part of humankind remembers those beliefs and fears the retribution that could be levied against them.

SECTION III

The Everyday Cat

The Uncommon Common Cat

The domesticated cat is a favorite companion animal with many people, and has been for centuries. The cat is a mammal and a carnivore. As a mammal, it is warm-blooded, has a skeleton, and a four-chambered heart; it gives birth to live young and suckles them. As a carnivore, the cat needs primarily meat and meat protein to survive; no cat can be a vegetarian.

There are no ordinary cats.

—COLETTE

There are about twenty-seven recognized pure breeds of shorthaired cats and seventeen breeds of longhaired ones. The most popular and common in households, however, is probably the mixed breed of common cat, who in actuality is as uncommon as the rest of the cat family. The lifespan of a non-pedigreed cat is normally longer than the life of a purebred cat. Whatever breed of cat a human cares for, that cat becomes part of the family, a loving companion, and a treasured friend.

The Origins of Cats

Scientists can't seem to agree how many genera cats should be divided into; some textbooks give six genera while others give four. The only thing they do agree on is that cheetahs, with their non-retractable claws, should have a genus of their own (*Acinonyx*).[1] The genus *Panthera* is given to the big cats that roar (lion, tiger, leopard, snow leopard, clouded leopard, and jaguar). The lynx, bobcat, and caracals belong to the genus *Lynx*. The small cats are placed in the genus *Felis*, with a couple of Asian cats undecided at this point.[2] The domesticated cat comes from the *Felis* genus.

The Roman Linnaeus first gave the Latin name *Felis catus* to both the European wild cat and the domestic breeds. This definition continued until 1777, when the naturalist Schreber separated the two breeds, giving the wild cat the name *Felis silvestris*.

The European forest cat (*Felis silvestris silvestris*) may have interbred with very early domesticated cats who were brought to Europe. It ranges from Portu-

gal and Britain in the west to Russia in the east. This cat has a sturdy body, a broad head, and a short bushy tail with a rounded tip. Its coat coloring is similar to the African wild cat—a washed-out tabby. It is very shy of humans and ferocious if caught; no one has ever managed to tame one of this species, even if taken as a kitten.

Today, a subspecies of this wild cat is found in the central and northern mountainous forests of the Scottish Highlands.

Although protected as an endangered species, the wild cat's numbers are in danger from illegal hunting.

The African wild cat (*Felis silvestris libyca*) is considered the most likely ancestor of the domesticated cat, which is known as *Felis silvestris catus*.

The African wild cat is also called the Egyptian cat or the Kaffir cat. It is found basically in the warm areas of Africa, Majorca, Corsica, Sardinia, Sicily, Crete, Syria, Arabia, the Middle East, and as far as India and Turkestan. It is

---

1. The cheetah also has a longer nose than other cats, so it can breathe easily when holding prey.
2. Muriel Beadle, *The Cat.*

larger than the house cat (about three feet long) and has faint tabby stripes on its tawny or light gray fur; the fur is tipped with flecks of black. These markings consist of four fairly dark lines on the back, while the light paws are ringed with black almost the length of the leg. Its body is less stocky than the modern cat, its head more delicate, and its tail long and thin. It is quite docile for a wild cat and can be easily tamed. The eyes of the African wild cat are rimmed with a dark color.[3] Its ear structure, both exterior and interior, seems to have developed for hearing in open spaces; this ear structure is basic in domesticated cats.

Pallas cat (*Felis manul*) comes from northern and central Asia. Because of its longhaired coat, some researchers believe it may have contributed to the ancestry of longhaired cats.[4]

The totally untamable European wild cat (*Felis silvestris silvestris*) probably interbred with domesticated cats when they were taken into Europe in the fourth century and may have contributed the dark tabby markings. Before this, the cat had only the lighter markings of the African wild cat. This grayish brown European feline is about the size of the African wild cat, but has a wider face, longer fur, and a bushier and blunter tail with black rings.

Except for the lion and cheetah, which live in family groups, cats tend to be natural loners. Although we consider the domesticated cat to be tame, it is quite capable of reverting to a feral[5] state and living in the wild without benefit of humans. Granted, the feral cat does not live as long as cats who are sheltered by humans; they die young of disease, malnutrition, and disaster.

Of all the cat family, the domesticated cat is also the most easily tamed, but doesn't transfer its loyalty easily. Although some cats will socialize with most visitors to a household, this isn't a trait that can be counted on. Almost all cats are highly discriminating about the humans with whom they associate. Some breeds of cats are noted for their attachment to a single human, disdaining all others.

Like humans and many other animals, the cat has an excellent internal clock. Cats prefer regularity in the schedules of their owners. In fact, they do better in orderly, predictable households. Cats who live with disorganized, unhappy families can even develop ulcers. Cats have a low tolerance to emotional stress.

This fixation with orderliness can play havoc during vacation, when the owner plans to sleep in and the cat is determined to keep the schedule as usual. Any cat owner can tell you that alarm clocks are optional, and be prepared for a week or two of upset when time is shifted to daylight savings and back.

---

3. One wonders if the ancient Egyptian women lined their eyes with dark kohl in imitation of this cat.
4. There are also other researchers who claim this is an impossibility.
5. "Feral" means a domesticated animal who reverts to a wild state.

The Body

Cats have amazing physical anatomy and characteristics. For example, cats have 244 bones in their skeleton, a bone structure vastly different from other mammals.[6] The longest recorded body length of a domestic cat is 41.5 inches. The cat's rounded head (large in proportion to its body), large forward-pointing eyes, and high brain case are the marks of a hunter. The seven vertebrae in its neck are much shorter than those of other animals. Since the cat only needs to digest meat, its intestines are short and simple.

Most cats are very intelligent, with an IQ far superior to other animals. In fact, a cat's memory can be up to two hundred times more retentive than that of a dog. Their abilities astound scientists and make fortunes for business people. However, cats exhibit their intelligence in their own way and at their own time and can't be trained in the same manner as dogs. Dr. Leon Smith is convinced that cats can be taught to do almost any type of work, an idea shared by Andre Marcal, a leading animal researcher in France.[7] However, most scientific training of cats seems to depend on the reward and punishment system, which many animal lovers personally oppose.

Its body is built for power and agility, from its narrow chest to its powerful hindquarters. When it crouches, it contracts two muscles: the hamstring (behind the thigh bone) and the tibialis (in front of the tibia and fibula bones).

The largest pure breed of domesticated cat is the Ragdoll, while the smallest is the Singapura. However, the difference in weight is seldom more than a dozen pounds, although I have had two mixed breed cats who were quite large—one weighing fourteen pounds, the other twenty-five.[8] A Siamese may weigh as little as five pounds, but most cats weigh between seven and twelve pounds, unless they have very large bone structure.

The difference between the longest and shortest of facial profiles is only about two inches. The only other major difference between cats—besides coloring, facial shapes, and ears—is that a few cats have extra toes.

Unless there is a physical ailment that upsets the sense of balance, a cat has the remarkable ability to keep its balance in situations that would have humans rigid

---

6. The skeletons of larger cats are similar to that of the domestic cat. The number of bones in the tail varies according to the species.
7. David Greene, *Your Incredible Cat*.
8. The heaviest domestic cat on record was a male tabby from Australia who weighed forty-seven pounds when he died in 1986. The lightest cat was a Siamese cross who weighed just one pound and twelve ounces at two years old.

with fear. Their ability to right themselves when falling, though, does not always keep them from harm. It all depends on the distance the cat falls, how it lands, and what it falls on. Some humans engage in the cruel practice of holding a kitten upside-down and dropping it, just to see how it will land. This can cause back injuries and certainly doesn't do much for establishing love and trust.

This ability to fall on their feet comes from the cat's flexing ability of the backbone; the primary reason for the flexibility is because the cat has five more vertebrae than humans. These extra vertebrae run back from the shoulder blades, giving the cat the ability to twist as much as 180 degrees.[9] Like other animals who are good runners, the cat has practically no collarbone. Its shoulder blades lie along the side of the chest. As a result of this skeletal structure, the cheetah, for example, can increase its walking stride by as much as four and one-half inches.

A relaxed cat will breathe twice as fast as a human—twenty-five to thirty times a minute. Their heartbeat is also twice as fast—110 to 140 times a minute. As a consequence, their half-pint of blood circulates completely through their body every eleven seconds. Because of this, cats are less likely than dogs or humans to have atherosclerosis or cerebral hemorrhages.

Cats have two blood types: A and B. These blood types are not the same as human blood groups. Most cats have A type blood. The white count of cats is much higher than that of humans; normally it is around 12,500. However, stress quickly can change the white count, as well as make the cat ill in other ways.

The tail of a cat can be long and thin or short, thick, and plume-like, depending on their hair length and the type of cat. Cats have marvelous control over this appendage, using it as a rudder when turning a corner at high speed or as a balance when walking on a narrow surface. It also comes in handy for keeping the nose warm or the light out of eyes when sleeping.

---

9. Zoologist Milton Hildebrand says that these extra vertebrae increase the speed of a cat's run.

Paws and Claws

The domesticated cat can walk easily along the narrow edge of a two-by-four piece of lumber, a traverse rod, or the head of your bed. Their feet are short, narrow in diameter, and have thin, light bones. Also, a cat's manner of walking allows its feet to land on almost the same print; the left and right paw prints line up right behind each other. A cat's feet are also without fur. The pads on the bottoms of the feet are like supple leather, enabling the animal to silently stalk, cushion landings, and stop suddenly in mid-run.

Except for the cheetah, members of the cat family have retractable front claws[10] that are usually pulled into a fold of skin around each toe. The curved fore claws are kept razor sharp by scratching to remove the outer sheaths, which are shed from time to time. Compressed on each side and hooked, these claws are the perfect cutting tool.

The hind claws are not as curved as the fore claws but are thicker and very dangerous weapons in defense against attacking animals. Cats chew the sheaths off the hind claws. Since the hind toes are less flexible than the front ones, and the claws are curved all in one direction, cats frequently have difficulty getting down trees, although they are excellent climbers for going up.

Deb Olson

Many people claim that the cat "hears" through the soles of its feet. They may not be far wrong in this assumption, for a great many cats can predict the approach of earthquakes or volcanic eruptions, as evidenced from their upset behavior prior to the natural disaster. During World War II, many cats in Britain could detect danger before the air raid sirens went off. They also appear to be able to predict atmospheric pressure changes.

---

10. A cat's claws are made of keratin, the same substance that forms human nails.

Some cats seem to have a homing ability enabling them to find their way home over vast distances.[11] These cats, and other animals, may have an unusual sensitivity to geomagnetic fields.

Cats don't perspire as humans do and must pant to cool the body. However, they do perspire on the bare pads of their feet when they become upset, frightened, or overheated. The pads of the feet are the only place a cat has sweat glands.

Teeth and Jaws

Domesticated cats have the fewest teeth of all the carnivores. Cats have thirty teeth, twelve fewer than a dog, with a pair of large, long, and sharp canine teeth in each jaw. Their back teeth mesh first when the jaw closes, giving a shearing action to the bite. They have no grinding teeth and must tear their food into small pieces to eat it.

Domesticated cats seem to have inborn skill in knowing how to deliver a death bite to such creatures as mice, rats, and such; this skill is brought into practice usually by the mother teaching her kittens. Ordinarily one quick, deep bite at the nape of the neck will dispatch the prey. If it remains alive, the cat will shake it vigorously sideways until the prey is dizzy and can be killed. Sometimes, with such animals as shrews and moles, the cat will give the animal a series of closed-paw blows to kill it. The shrew in particular is extremely ferocious and has a disagreeable odor; it is very seldom that a cat will actually eat one.

If your cat has access to the outdoors, or if a mouse gets into the house, you may be presented with a gift of dispatched prey from time to time—sometimes even a live one. There is some debate on why this occurs or even if it is intentional. However, I'm certain that cat owners will agree that cats present these gifts for definite reasons. They may be offerings because the cat considers its human to be part of its family. Sometimes they are peace offerings after they have been scolded. But other times, I feel certain that the cat is full of unfailing hope that one day we will learn to hunt. A cat owner should never scold the cat who brings in its prey, for it is only following its natural instincts. The gift of prey also shows that the cat considers you worthy of being cared for. However well-fed the cat may be, it will hunt.

We had a black, silver, and buff tom for seventeen years whose name was Flash. As each of the grandchildren became old enough to walk, they were dutifully presented on more than one occasion with an injured but live mouse. We

11. Sheila Burnford, *The Incredible Journey*.

would hear Flash singing long before he came through the cat door, but he always managed to evade capture to drop the mouse directly in front of the baby. Then he would sit back and watch as the adults frantically raced around, trying to catch the mouse. The children, of course, were too young to be frightened, only vastly entertained by the suddenly active adults. The only prey Flash refused to share were lizards. He also had a policy that any mouse once within the house was mine, and he firmly refused to catch it.

Most naturally wild cats will pull off the feathers and at least most of the fur before they eat their prey. The domesticated cat, however, is more tolerant. They generally eat their prey, beginning with the head and leaving the gallbladder and stomach for the human to dispose of.

Cats require more fat and protein than dogs—almost four times as much—which is why they should never be fed dog food. However, they do not require as much as many people think. Cats need about thirty percent protein in their diet; the cat foods with up to fifty and sixty percent protein are unnecessary.[12] The old belief that cats crave and must have fish is also wrong. Spoiled fish or certain types of fish can cause diseases; it is best to get a commercial cat food that has some fish in it. And, contrary to the newest fad going around, cats cannot live on a vegetarian diet; they will become very sick and die a painful death. As carnivores, they naturally must have protein in their diet.

---

12. A good source of information on the subject of proper cat feeding is your local veterinarian or veterinary schools.

Although milk is a source of protein, a great many adult cats don't have the necessary enzymes to digest it; instead it gives the cat diarrhea. Besides, too much calcium fed to kittens can cause bone disease.

The Ears

The ears of a cat are extremely sensitive, far more sensitive than the ears of humans or dogs. They dislike loud sounds, probably because it causes them pain. They hear about two octaves higher than humans do; their higher level of hearing is also better than that of a dog. In fact, they can hear sounds up to 100,000 cycles per second, the pitch of mouse noises.[13]

Experiments have shown that cats can distinguish between sources of sounds when the sounds are as close as three inches apart. With all this ultra-sensitive and discriminatory hearing, any cat owner knows that they can also ignore you whatever the distance.

Some cats seem to prefer women to men. Perhaps this is because the typical female voice is much higher pitched and closer in quality to that of the cat itself.

The cat's ears are very flexible. When determining the source of a sound, the cat can either turn its head or one or both ears. This movement allows the cat to use the ears as funnels, directing the sound onto the eardrum. Sometimes, this ear-twisting movement reminds one of independent radar screens as they adjust singularly and then together to determine what is causing the noise. They can also hear another cat walking on carpet, even if the cat is not in view.

The long hair inside the cat's ears enables it to catch the tiniest vibrations in the air. This alerts it to movements it hasn't even seen.

Cats react to certain sounds more than others. A cat can be totally relaxed or asleep, but if it hears the live-recorded sounds of birds on TV or stereo, it will be awake in a second, looking for the birds it is certain are in the house. The meow of a cat on TV may bring it to investigate, either ready to fight or full of curiosity. Some music will send a cat into a panic, while other renditions will send it off to sleep.

I have a CD titled "Lunar Goddess" that has real wolves howling on it. The first time I played it, Callisto circled the room at high speed, hair raised, eyes big, belly to the floor, and growling. After that first experience, she now indignantly leaves the room if that particular music is played.

---

13. Over fifty years ago, Drs. Morin and Bachrach discovered that a certain note would cause younger cats to defecate and older ones to become excited; Gary Brodsky, *The Mind of the Cat.*

Fur and Whiskers

Even the hair on cats is more than it seems at first glance. This fur coat insulates the cat in both hot and cold weather, protects its skin from scratches and scrapes, carries its odor, and is another part of its sensory apparatus. Wild cats basically have two layers of hair: a warm layer of down hair underneath and a resilient outer coat.

Most cats have three types of hair in their coat; however, there are a few breeds that have only two, like the wild cats, and a few that have only one. The long hairs on a domesticated cat's fur are called primary or guard hairs; these hairs grow from individual follicles. There are two types of secondary hairs—awn hairs and down hairs—which grow in groups. Awn hairs are usually medium in length and rather bristly tipped. The down hairs are the shortest and are usually very fine and sometimes crinkled. A cat can have as many as 200 hairs per square millimeter of skin.

There are about seven to twenty-five touch spots per square centimeter of skin on a cat. This sensitivity causes the cat's skin to ripple when the fur is disturbed, such as flicking drops of water onto the cat.

The whiskers of a cat are known as vibrissae. They are of varying lengths and grow on the upper lip, under the chin, over the eyes, and on the cheeks; they are also found on the backs of the forelegs. These whiskers are so sensitive that they don't need to touch something to know it is there. Using the vibrissae, the cat can detect tiny variations in the air currents that flow around solid objects. The vibrissae or whiskers are aids to vision and hearing. They also help the cat determine how close its body is to something in the dark.

The loose skin on the back, and especially on the back of the neck, is generally five times thicker than the skin on the legs. In fact, on old, unneutered toms the skin on the back of the neck can be as much as a quarter of an inch thick. This looseness and thickness of skin enables the cat to escape predators—instead of getting a body grip, the predator ends up with a mouthful of loose skin. This looseness allows the cat to twist and rake at the eyes with its claws.

The Nose, Tongue, and Scenting Abilities

Around the nose the skin is lightly furred. The cat's nose has nineteen million nerves just for smelling, compared to the human's five million.[14] This area, plus the nose itself, is extremely sensitive to temperature changes. The upper lip itself can detect an increase in warmth of less than two degrees and an increase in coolness of less than one degree.

Dr. Hans Precht, a German animal expert, discovered that it is possible to tell the temperature of a room by the way a cat is curled when sleeping. In a room under fifty-five degrees Fahrenheit, a cat will be tightly curled with its tail completely over its nose; at sixty to sixty-five degrees, the cat will be semi-curled, with its nose uncovered; at seventy degrees and above, the cat will be stretched out completely.

The cat's tongue is an amazing organ. It curls inward when the cat drinks, forming a little spoon; every four or five laps, the cat will swallow the liquid. The tongue is thin and pliant at the edges, but thickens in the center. It is also covered with dozens of little rough projections with hooked ends extending backward. These rough protrusions can rasp meat off bones and remove loose fur.

Scientists say that cats have only four tastes: sweet, sour, salt, and bitter. They can also detect the difference between plain water and other liquids. Some cats develop tastes for specific foods.

Traditionally, cats are supposed to like catnip, and some say valerian. However, in 1963 scientists discovered that cats inherit the catnip response, which explains why some cats are crazy about the herb and others ignore it. Cats can detect the odor of catnip[15] in the air in as little as one part per billion. Most cats will roll in the catnip and inhale its odor to get their temporary "high." However, once in a while a cat will carefully select one leaf and eat it.

All cats have a peculiar habit of opening their mouths and wrinkling their noses when they detect certain odors. This reaction is called flehmen. Many people think this is caused by the odor itself, as when humans smell something disagreeable. However, this isn't true. The cat has an auxiliary scent gland far back on the roof of the mouth called the Jacobson's organ. This organ is connected to two different parts of the hypothalamus, while the olfactory cells of the nose are connected to a different part of the brain.

When a cat flehms, it starts by smelling or licking an object, often a sex gland, then raising its head and inhaling through the mouth. The lips pull back and

14. David Alderton, *Pockets Cats.*
15. The active ingredient in catnip which attracts cats is nepetalactone.

the nose wrinkles, giving an expression of disgust. At the same time the tongue flicks against the roof of the mouth, depositing the odor on the duct of the Jacobson's organ. This helps the cat to analyze any substance that might be of significance to it.

Cats have also been known to snore. The snore may only be a tiny buzzing-like rattle, just at the edge of your hearing, or a noise loud enough to wake you from a sound sleep. As with humans, a cat's snore is very individual.

The Eyes

The eyes of a cat can be round, almond-shaped, or anywhere in between. Cat's eyes are the largest of any mammal in relation to their body size. Although they can't see in total darkness, as alluded to in folklore, they can see in darkness that would leave a human blind and bumping into things. Their pupils can contract to as little as a bare slit or expand to such an extent that only a tiny rim of color is showing. When opened to their fullest, the eye allows all possible light to enter. Any night hunter will have larger eyes than other carnivores.

©Ron Sanford / International Stock

Night shine as seen from the eyes of a bobcat

As sharp as their eyesight appears to be, cats are farsighted. They see better between seven and twenty feet than up close, such as within a few inches.

The cat has a third eyelid called the haw or nictitating membrane. This thin, whitish lid is situated at the inner corner of the eye. It is automatically activated to protect the eye from damage and to lubricate the corneal surface by evenly distributing tears.

Scientists are beginning to change their opinion about cats being color blind; at one time they said cats only saw in shades of gray. Any cat owner can tell you that cats can distinguish between colors if they want to.

One year I bought our grandsons birthday gifts and left them in a bright red plastic bag until they could be delivered. Beowulf wanted in that bag in the worst way. Finally, when he was out of the room, I placed it on top of a tall bookcase. As soon as he came back, however, he looked around and immediately spotted the bag.

The eyes of a cat are very large in relation to the rest of the head, and they glow with an exotic light at night. This night shine is different in cats according to the color of their eyes. Cats with gold to copper-colored eyes will reflect a yellow-green or blue-green shine, while those with blue eyes will reflect red. The paranoid witch hunters and their church supporters believed that this night shine was a reflection of the fires in hell. Other old tales say that this night shine is really luminous jewels inside the cat's head.

This night shine or eye shine is caused by light reflecting off the guanin on the back of a cat's eyes. Guanin are the masses of tiny metallic-like particles coated on the lining at the back of the eye. When struck by light, the guanin particles amplify and brighten any picture focused on the retina. After a certain amount of time, these particles retreat into their cells and the eye shine ceases.

Purring

There is an old folk tale about how cats got their purr. Once a princess had to spin 10,000 skeins of linen thread in thirty days or her true love would die. She asked three cats to help her. By working day and night, the job was finished on time and the princess united with her love. The reward to the cats was their purr, an imitation of the spinning wheel's whirring sound.

Cats usually purr when they are contented with life and feel safe. However, some cats also purr when they are frightened or badly hurt.[16] Newborn kittens use their mother's purring as a kind of homing beacon so they can find her if they stray from the nest. The kittens learn to purr by imitating her.

---

16. Some scientists and cat-people think that perhaps this purring when scared or injured is a cat's way of recalling kitten-hood, when the mother purred to her babies and kept them safe.

A biomedical research team at Tulane University discovered that the cat's purr doesn't come from the voice box and diaphragm, as previously thought, but from the muscles around this voice box. The purring, which sounds like a rolled R, only comes from the mouth and nose of the cat although it vibrates through the chest. Almost all wild cats can only purr when they inhale, but domestic cats can purr when they inhale and exhale.

The purr is a very individual thing; each cat's purr is distinctive in tone, loudness, and when it chooses to do this. Some cats rarely purr, while others purr most of the time. As to loudness, I have had cats you couldn't hear purr and knew they were purring only when you put your hand on them. But our cat Flash sounded like a diesel truck shifting gears when going up a hill. If Flash wanted you to get up, there was no way you could sleep through his purring. He

had his purr refined into an art form, but he rarely talked to you unless he felt he had something to gripe about.

People think that cats purr only when they are contented. However, the purr is also used during other situations to let you know the cat wishes your company or help. A sick cat will sometimes purr to let the owner know it needs help. Mother cats purr to let their kittens know it is time to eat. Cats often purr when they lie beside the owner who is not feeling well. Sometimes cats will purr to themselves when they are left alone.

Breeding and Territory

In anatomy and behavior, the domesticated cat has remained very close to the form of its ancestors. Most of the changes it has undergone are superficial. The coat color, hair length, and size (now slightly smaller than wild cats) have been modified, for example. The domestic cat is the only member of the cat family that lives and breeds freely within human societies.[17]

---

17. The cheetah can be tamed, although it never loses its wild nature. For 1,000 years, in India and the Middle East, the cheetah was used for hunting, especially in the pursuit of gazelles.

The breeding cycle is another change; wild cats only breed once in the spring. Domestic cats can breed several times a year. Small felines can breed before they are a year old, while the big cats usually don't have the first litter until they are three years old.[18] It is possible that a litter of kittens may have more than one father.

It takes sixty-five days for the unborn kittens of a domestic cat to develop enough to be born.[19] The period for the big wild cats is 115 days. Newborn kittens are helpless, huddling together for warmth and depending on the mother's licking action to enable them to urinate and defecate. They are also blind and deaf for over a week; all kittens have blue eyes when they are born. Although domestic kittens are independent at three months of age, those in the wild may stay with their mother for up to two years. The domestic mother will usually wean her kittens at about six to eight weeks, while wild cubs take twice as long.

Kittens begin to practice their prey-catching stalking and pouncing when they are about three weeks old. The most important part is the neck-bite, which cats use to kill rodents and other small prey. Using each other or small objects for practice, they gradually become more adept at hunting skills. If their mother is a hunter and has access to the outdoors, she will probably bring the kittens an injured but live rodent and further teach them the refined skills of hunting and killing prey.

Determining the sex of a small kitten can be difficult, even for those who are very familiar with cats. I have had success using an old formula called "the dot and dash." If you lift the kitten's tail, you will see what looks like a dot and dash. With female kittens the dot and dash are farther apart than on males.

Since female cats can become pregnant before they are a year old, and males can be sexually active, it is best to have females spayed and males neutered at around six months of age. If all cat owners would take this responsibility seriously, we would have fewer heartbreaking scenes at the local animal shelters.

---

18. One tabby cat from Texas had a total of 420 kittens. The oldest cat to have kittens was recorded in 1987 as having two kittens at the age of thirty; *Pockets Cats*.

19. The average litter of a domestic cat is four or five. However, the record is held by a Burmese who had nineteen kittens in one litter.

The correct word for a group of cats is *clowder,* an old dialect word for *clutter.* But a group of kittens is called a *kyndyll* or kindle of cats. This probably comes from the old verb "to kindle," which means "to give birth to young." Personally, I've always referred to a friendly group of cats as a "cuddle of cats."

Grown domesticated cats look on their human's home as their nest and their territory long after they are kittens. They also look on their human owners as pseudo-parents and sometimes as siblings. This idea of territorial rights often causes problems when bringing new cats into a household. You can expect a period where the old cats will dislike the new ones, whatever you do. Be prepared for about two weeks of everybody hating each other.

Cats use their claws for more than defense or repelling unwanted attention. Remember, cats seldom scratch anyone they don't mean to scratch. As every cat owner knows, they go through spells of scratching that can instantly shred furniture, have the curtains hanging in ribbons, or make a hole in a cardboard box full of computer paper. This type of scratching is a natural instinct to mark territory. The scratches themselves are a territorial sign to other felines just as the urine spray markings are, but the scent glands between the toes reinforce this marking.

Some cat owners have their felines declawed to prevent major damage to belongings. However, having had this done once to my cats, I don't think I would again; declawing is the equivalent of having your fingernails removed. Carefully cutting the very tips of the claws with nail clippers can prevent most, if not all, of scratching damage. Also, providing your cats with a sisal scratch-pole or the more favorably accepted cardboard scratchers will allow the cat to satisfy its natural scratching instinct without causing damage to the furniture.

Deb Weichel

An invitingly furry cuddle of cats

Diseases and Illnesses

A healthy domesticated cat can live from ten to twenty years of age, although a few live even longer. The record is held by a British tabby who died in 1957 at the age of thirty-four.

Although cats have excellent resistance to hardening of the arteries and most infections, they are very susceptible to bacterial contamination of wounds. They also can suffer from allergies, arthritis, asthma, cancer, cataracts, diabetes, diarrhea, eczema, parasitic infections, toothache, urinary tract problems, and diseases caused by viruses (the most dreaded and deadly).

The top virus infection is known as cat distemper, feline enteritis, or feline panleukopenia. At least half of the infected cats die of this gastrointestinal illness. It shows up every year in the U.S., being worse between December and February.

The most serious and deadly virus disease is rabies, which can easily be prevented by vaccination. The virus is transmitted by an infected animal through the saliva. However, people are more likely to get rabies from a dog than from a cat.

Leukemia (cancer of the blood) is two and one-half times more common among cats than humans. Unfortunately, there is no cure. It can, however, be prevented by vaccination. One problem with leukemia is that you can get what appears to be a perfectly healthy cat. Unless you have the animal tested for leukemia—a prerequisite before vaccination for this disease—you have no way to know until the cat becomes inexplicably ill.

One of the big complaints by some people is that cats can give you catscratch fever. This disease, which usually appears as fever and redness and swelling of scratches, is wrongly named because you can get this fever without being bitten or scratched by a cat.

Like humans, cats are susceptible to upper respiratory infections caused by viruses. These are usually feline pneumonitis, rhinotracheitis, and picornavirus infection, and they also can catch colds. The expression "sick as a cat" is an appropriate description of a cat with a cold, who can be as miserable as we are with the same illness.

A great many cat diseases can be prevented by vaccinations given by your veterinarian. If you truly love your cat, you should take it for yearly check-ups and the appropriate vaccinations. You should also be aware that if you allow your cat to roam freely outdoors, you are taking chances of them catching diseases, including a form of AIDS for which there is no cure, from other cats, whose owners are less inclined to give them good veterinary care.

Allowing a cat outdoors also exposes it to other hazards. It can be killed by cars, malicious humans, or dogs; get infected bites from other cats or wild animals; or pick up a number of intestinal parasites, not to mention the ever-present flea, who carries the tapeworm. In cold weather a cat can also suffer frostbite on its ears, feet, tail, and face within a short period of time.

Cat Welfare

Many cats are accidentally poisoned because their owners are careless. Two of the worst poisons are disinfectants and pesticides, especially poisons used to kill mice and other vermin. Any weed killer, furniture spray, insect killer, or disinfectant that can get onto a cat's fur and be licked off will cause a painful death. One of the most deadly poisons is common antifreeze; cats like the flavor, and it only takes a tiny amount to kill a cat. Chocolate can also be deadly to a cat.

You should also never give a cat acetaminophen, alcohol, or aspirin. These substances can kill. So can carelessly dropped prescription drugs, especially those used to treat heart conditions. Any other prescription or over-the-counter medication used by humans should be treated as a poison to cats. Even such things as shaving lotions, coffee, suntan lotions, and fingernail polish remover are very dangerous.

Several houseplants are also dangerous. Daffodil, dieffenbachia (dumb cane), Easter lily, English ivy, holly, iris, mistletoe, oleander, philodendron, and rhododendron are toxic to cats and other animals. Growing oat grass for your cat will give it something to nibble on besides your plants, but is not a cure-all. The best method is simply to not have any dangerous plants around.

If you suspect your cat has eaten some poisonous substance, don't wait. Get it to the veterinarian immediately!

A few of the danger signals of a sick cat are vomiting, blood in the stool, a swelling or tenderness in the abdomen, a warm dry nose, refusal to eat or drink, listlessness, crying when urinating, or the unnatural appearance of the third eyelid. It is normal for cats to vomit on occasion, particularly if they have eaten grass. However, if any of these symptoms last more than twenty-four hours, you should immediately take the cat to a veterinarian. Even though many vets will recommend that you take the cat's temperature by inserting a thermometer into the rectum, I prefer to use the new digital ear thermometers. If you carefully work the thermometer into the ear canal, you should be able to get an accurate reading. The normal temperature for a cat is about 100 degrees Fahrenheit.

Leaving for vacation or a necessary out-of-town trip makes it imperative that you consider the welfare of your cats while you are gone. Never leave your cat home alone for more than three days at the most, and only if you put out several dishes of food and water. It is better to find a cat-loving sitter who gets along with your cats in particular, and have them stay at your house. Barring this, consider a kennel for cats, preferably one that doesn't take in dogs; barking dogs leave cats with the feeling that a pack is just around the corner and could get them at any moment.

If you are thinking of taking your cat along on your trip, please consider that most cats don't like to travel, aren't fond of cars or strange places, and are apt to slip out the first open door and be lost forever.

When friends or family come for a visit, particularly if there will be many strangers present, it is best if you confine your cats to a room with litter box, fresh water, food, and most of all a piece of your unwashed clothing that is ripe with your scent. Very few cats aren't upset by strangers and want to be in the midst of everything. However, most cats are uncomfortable in such situations and would rather feel secure behind a closed door, sniffing at one of your raunchy old T-shirts.

There is no such thing as a common cat. All cats are unique, just as all humans are unique and different. Even within the same breed there are differences in personalities. Treat your cat as you would a special friend, and you will have a concerned, loving companion who cares for you whatever the rest of the world thinks.

Cat Talk

10

The domesticated cat is an amazingly expressive animal. If you are observant, you can easily determine what your cat is trying to communicate to you. Cats have numerous ways of expressing themselves, just as humans do: tail movements, facial expressions, ears, eyes, body language, and of course the famous meow in all its inflections and volumes.

A cat is a lion in a jungle of small bushes.

—INDIAN PROVERB

The Tail

Cats' tails are amazingly animated and expressive appendages. They can make the tail say just about anything they want, from greeting to insult.

When greeting a person or other animal whom it likes, the cat will raise its tail straight up; the tail may quiver with delight just before the cat rubs against the person or other animal and winds the tail about the object

137

being greeted. This rubbing has another objective: to leave the cat's scent. Cats don't rub against anyone they don't like.

Rubbing against people or objects is a signal to other cats, "This person or object is mine or in my territory." If you have more than one cat in your household, you have probably seen one cat after another mark the same object, a sort of declaration of "You aren't the only cat this belongs to."

If the cat is interested in getting acquainted with a person or other cat, but a little hesitant, the tip of the tail may tilt to one side.

If the cat faces possible conflict with another cat (and sometimes with a human), the tail will be vertical and slightly bushed out. This is a signal that says, "You are in my territory, and I plan to run you out." Next, there is usually a staring match, accompanied by growls and hisses, with the tail whipping from side to side as the tension gets stronger.[1] It often ends with one cat attacking, tail streaming out behind.

The cat uses a certain flick of the tail while facing away from the human or animal whom it wishes to insult. The tail flick is the same as a human thumbing their nose or using a more rude gesture.

When my neighbors had to be out of town for a few days, I fed their cats—a Siamese named Maggie and an Abyssinian called Elliot. Maggie was very shy, seldom coming near the food until I was a safe distance away. Elliot, however, became my friend, always greeting me at the door and being under my feet until I left. When the owners returned, it became a different relationship. Each time I visited, Elliot would walk away and twitch his tail. Never having experienced this before, I innocently asked if he had fleas. Suzanne laughed and informed me I had received the ultimate cat insult, meaning "I want nothing more to do with you." So I was introduced to the insulting tail-twitch.

If one is observant and aware, every movement or position of the tail can tell us about the emotional state of the cat. When the tail swishes violently from side to side, the cat is very angry. If it is lowered and fuzzed, it shows fear. A stiff, upright tail that looks like a bottle brush is a warning of aggression. When the tail is relaxed with just the tip twitching back and forth, the cat is irritated and

---

1. The actress Sarah Bernhardt once said that she wished she could have a cat's tail grafted onto her spine so she could lash it when angry.

will probably slap you if you persist in annoying it. A stiff tail that is held upright and quivers is a special greeting for loved people, usually the owner.

Tail-less cats, such as the Manx, Japanese Bobtail, American Bobtail, and Cymric, do not appear to be hampered in their balance or expression of moods by lack of a tail or a shortened tail. Instead, they rely on facial expressions, body language, vocal tones, and ear positions.

The Ears

The cat can convey a number of messages with the position of its ears. Few humans will mistake the message when a cat has flattened its ears back. The cat is clearly stating its nervousness and anger at being threatened in some way. The ears will be sharply pointed forward when interested in something, especially if that something is possible prey to be hunted. When peering through windows or over grass, the hunting cat's ears will bend forward, presenting the least possible silhouette to the victim.

Body Language

Body language was used by cats long before humans became interested in the subject. A cat that lies on its back with belly exposed is expressing total trust in the humans within its domain. By the same token, a cat will lick excessively if it feels anxious, just as a human might bite their fingernails.

Rubbing around a human's legs is the equivalent of saying, "Hello, I'm glad to see you." This rubbing motion also leaves the cat's subtle scent, thus marking you as his or her personal property. This same rubbing motion, especially with the chin, is used by cats to mark every box, bed, piece of furniture, and the corners of woodwork within its territory.

Body language extends to the kneading on your legs when sitting in your lap. Usually this method of communication says that the cat is contented and feels free to express its affection for the person involved. It may also be reminiscent of the action of kittens against their mother while they nurse. The honored person is often biting a lip to keep from yelling as the claws are delicately placed on nerve endings in the leg.

However, a few cats have taken the kneading process into the realms of sarcasm. Flash used this method to get rid of unwelcome guests. If he felt they were staying too long, he got onto their laps and began his "surgery of the leg nerves" with great concentration and determination.

Some cats who have been scolded or laughed at will sulk by turning their backs on the offenders, while others will turn their backs and groom themselves as if nothing happened. Some cats, however, are known for waiting hours to get revenge for what they consider to be an insult.

Flash hated being laughed at and seemed to know just what method of revenge would get to an offending human the best. He would wait for hours, giving the appearance of having completely forgotten about the insult. Then, when you least expected it, he would sneak into a dark room and wait. In the second just before you flipped the light switch, he would leap out and grab you around the leg, then run by you as fast as he could go. When our oldest grandson was very small, he refused to go into any dark room unless an adult went in first.

The normal licking and grooming between cats is a sign of affection. Cats don't lick other cats or people whom they are not fond of. The lick is an expression of trust and complete acceptance.

There has been much discussion among cat lovers about the cat's ability to smile. One usually thinks of the overzealous Cheshire Cat from *Alice's Adventures in Wonderland* when discussing cat smiles. Unlike dogs, who can be taught

to draw back their lips in a pseudo-smile, cats actually can turn up the corners of their mouth in a smug grin. Perhaps observation of the cat's smile was the origin of the expression of someone looking "like the cat who ate the canary." This smile can be observed when a cat is relaxed and pleased with the situation or when it is engaged in some pleasant dream.

The Cheshire Cat's famous grin in *Alice's Adventures in Wonderland*

The Eyes

Cats also communicate their feelings through the eyes. A staring match between two cats on opposite sides of a room or across a yard is like a laser beam. Volumes are said in this unblinking gaze. Cats can out-stare almost any creature, including a human. However, if you are trying to make friends with a cat, you should never stare back at it. The best results come from turning your eyes elsewhere and blinking. To the cat, this is a sign that you are not threatening their position in their own territory.

When a cat is contented and relaxed, its eyes will be partly or fully closed, and it may be purring. If its attention has been aroused, but the cat isn't certain about what it sees, the eyes will be wide open and the gaze riveted on the object or animal; the ears will be perked up to take in all possible sound for information.

Ancient Chinese picture-writing used drawings of cats' eyes to illustrate the passage of time. A thin line meant noon (the brightest part of the day) and a circle stood for midnight (the darkest part).

Vocal Sounds

The most common aspect of cat speech is the meow, mew, or *mmmmrrr* sound. Kittens will meow from a very young age, relying on this form of communication with their mother. Some cats talk in this manner more than others, and some are quite eloquent in the speech-range of the meow.[2]

Dr. Mildren Moelk, an American researcher working in Rochester, New York, has spent years on cat language. She has determined that, although cats use their larynx as humans do, they don't use the tip of the tongue in shaping sounds. The cat produces thirteen distinct vowel sounds and seven to eight consonant sounds in speaking. She also has detected three main groups of sounds, modulated by mouth position. Murmurs are made with a closed mouth; calls are formed by an open mouth that slowly closes while the sound continues; cries are issued with a tense mouth constantly open.[3]

The full meow to a human is primarily a statement of "listen to me when I'm telling you about my day" or "I want you to do something for me right now," while the more delicate mew is a punctuation of communication. The murmuring *mmmmrrr* sound (at least with Callisto) means "Stop playing ignorant and come do what I want, pretty please." The only time Valkyrie uses her tiny, nearly inaudible mew is to say, "I feel like playing."

Beowulf talks in a loud, insistent variety of meows for a number of reasons; he may be telling you about the day's events, complaining that the girls have gone off and he can't find them, he's hungry, he's glad to see you, or, as my husband says, just general griping. When he uses his drawn-out, louder call, he is trying to find out where everybody is.

The griping, complaining, or protesting sound is usually a single, high note broken into short syllables. This is used when a cat feels it has a legitimate complaint that is not being taken care of. Since cats love the dramatic, they seldom miss an opportunity to let the whole house know when they feel their rights and needs are being ignored.

Cats save a special tiny chattering meow for small creatures they consider exciting to hunt. This meow is usually expressed with nose pressed to the window while butterflies and birds are flitting by. They will also utter this tiny teeth-clacking noise when they are pursuing such little creatures as flies, gnats, bees, and crickets.

---

2. Tradition says that a cat's meow has sixty-three notes.
3. David Greene, *Your Incredible Cat.*

Growling is generally one of the very last warnings you get when a cat is telling you to leave it alone. The animal will ordinarily warn you with a loud hiss first. Instantly after the growl, the offender will be given a swat with claws out, usually directly on the nose; this same procedure is used by the mother to correct offending offspring. Growling is a sign of deep irritation, often accompanied by ears flattened back to the skull and a swishing tail. Most feline mothers (called queens in domestic cats) will growl in order to get the undivided attention of their rambunctious kittens.

Hissing is another warning signal from a cat. The hiss reminds one of a snake; some researchers think the cat purposely uses the hiss to imitate snakes. I've heard tiny kittens hiss, followed by a loud, explosive sound like a pistol shot; this combination warning startles approaching humans and allows the kitten to escape.

When it comes to hair-raising vocal sounds, the feline family wins hands down. The sight, let alone the sounds, of two opposing domesticated male cats is drama at its highest, right down to the smallest movement. The hair on their backs stands up in a ridge, with tail fuzzed out to its fullest and whipping from side to side. The ears are slicked back, the head thrust forward, while the legs perform a stiff dance in slow motion. They will hiss, yowl, slobber, and growl, each vocal challenge trailing off into a high-pitched scream. They grind their teeth, drool, and scream their challenges until they both have worked up their courage. When finally head to head, the males will freeze for a moment before they spring into a no-holds-barred free-for-all. This action is repeated until one male decides to call it quits.

Female cats will protect their territory, but in not nearly the dramatic way of the males. They usually come to an unspoken agreement with other females that keeps fights to a minimum. If they have kittens nearby, females will take on any trespasser or aggressor without warning.

An example of this occurred when a friend's two female cats had litters the same week. The dog next door had been a constant irritation, for he always came into Ann's yard to do his smelly business. But one day his visits ended

abruptly, and he never returned. Both mother cats were feeding and grooming their kittens in a corner of the laundry room when they suddenly froze, looked at each other for an instant, and in perfect harmony tore through the house and out the cat door. The dog, who was preparing to do his business on the flowers again, never knew what hit him. Without a sound of warning, both females hit the dog's back at the same instant. Only when aboard and all eight feet sending up a cloud of dog hair did they begin screaming at the top of their lungs. The dog shot out of the yard and down the alley at top speed with the two cats still on his back. The cats came strolling back in a few moments to rejoin their kittens as if nothing had happened, but with a look of "Well, that's taken care of." The dog never returned.

It is important to establish communication with your cat. This is best accomplished through gentle touches and actually speaking to it. Cats don't respond well to loud, angry tones and physical punishment. If your cat is misbehaving, it is not being contrary for no reason. Cats need, and thrive on, positive communication with their owners. Contented, happy cats are less likely to develop destructive habits, such as ripping up your new sofa.

Like humans, cats do have crises points in their lives and need the reassurance and understanding of their owners. The birth process can make a new mother cat nervous and tense, particularly if you allow visitors near her nest for the first week or so. Give her lots of privacy, but spend time reassuring her also.

Another stressful situation is the loss of a companion, whether another cat or a human in the household. Cats do grieve, much as we do, and need to be consoled. Often the surviving cat will follow its owner around, meowing pitifully and begging for much extra attention and love for a period of time. If the loss is a human one, both you and the cat can comfort each other. Cats who have formed a close bond with their human are very sensitive to the emotions of that human. Illness or sadness will bring your purring bundle of fur running to spend as much time by your side as you need.

11

Other Members of the Cat Family

There are many species of small to medium-sized cat other than the ones talked about in the last chapter. There are also the larger felines, who fascinate many people. Unfortunately, this fascination has led to the slaughter of many cats for their fur and their bones, which are believed to have curative powers.

If a man could be crossed with the cat, it would improve the man but deteriorate the cat.

—MARK TWAIN

There are two definite behaviors separating the big cats and the smaller ones. In both the Old and New Worlds, the big cats leave their feces uncovered and lie with their front legs straight out before them. The small cats of the Old World curl their paws under their chest when reclining and cover their feces. The instinct with the feces probably is determined by the size of the cat. After all, the larger ones are strong enough that they don't care who knows they are around; the smaller ones are using their cunning to avoid predators.

African Golden Cat

About twice the size of a domestic cat, this animal ranges through the mountains and deciduous forest of central and western Africa. Its short, dense coat comes in shades of brown, red, and gray; spotting is common. The ears are black on the backsides. The head is small, the legs fairly long, and the body sturdy. About thirty-five inches in length, this cat can weigh an average of thirty-four pounds.

The African golden cat (*Felis aurata*) is seen infrequently as it hunts during twilight, dusk, and at night. Some of the Pygmy tribes consider the tail of this cat a good luck symbol, especially when hunting large animals.

Black-Footed Cat

Smaller than a housecat, this animal (*Felis nigripes*) is the smallest wild feline in the world. The average length is only about sixteen inches and the weight about four pounds. This cat has rows of round dark spots on a sandy-brown coat; the tail (about seven inches long), however, has black bars and a black tip. The small ears are black on the outer side with a little dash of white.

©Zoological Society of San Diego

Black-footed cat (*Felis nigripes nigripes*)

This wild feline is found throughout south, southeast, and southwest Africa and through the Kalahari Desert. It seems to prefer the arid, desert areas. Known as the *Sebulabulakwana*[1] in Africa, the ferocious black-footed cat feeds on small mammals, rodents, birds, and reptiles. It has been known to kill an animal four times its size.

Bobcat

Known scientifically as *Felis rufus*, the bobcat resembles the lynx. In fact, the bobcat is also called the bay lynx and the American wild cat. It is thinner and smaller than the lynx, with smaller feet and ears that have less of a tuft on them. The short tail hampers the bobcat in communications, but it makes up for this disadvantage by the use of its long, black ear tufts. Its basic coat color can range from yellow-brown to buff or gray. It is spotted with black, with a black streak on its head. About twenty-one inches high, the bobcat seldom weighs more than thirty-two pounds. This feline is the only wild cat that can purr while inhaling or exhaling, the same as a domesticated cat.

The most numerous of North American wild cats, the bobcat can be found from southern Canada, through the U.S., and into parts of Mexico. They hunt at night, using their extraordinary vision to catch rodents, birds, and deer. The bobcat prowls a smaller personal territory than the lynx, only ranging long distances from its den during hard times.

Caracal Lynx

The caracal[2] (*Felis caracal*) is only about twenty-nine inches long and weighs about thirty-eight pounds, but is very powerful. This animal is similar to the lynx in body, except that it has a long tail and different coat markings. Its dense, short fur is in various shades of reddish brown, with white marks on the chin, throat, belly, and around the eyes. A thin black line runs from the nose and over the eyes.

The caracal is found throughout Africa and southern Asia, primarily in arid land, but not in the deserts. Known also as the desert lynx, this animal hunts during both day and night. It is an expert climber and the fastest feline of its size.

---

1. James Johnson, *The Mini-Atlas of Cats.*
2. The name *Caracal* comes from a Turkish word *karakal*, which means "black ear."

Cheetah

Today, the cheetah (*Acinonyx jubatus*) is primarily found in Africa, although it does have a limited range in Asia; it is extinct in India. This unique member of the feline family has non-retractable claws. Its long legs and lean body make it an extremely fast runner for short periods of time; it has been known to reach speeds of forty-five mph in three seconds and sixty mph about two seconds later.[3] The cheetah uses its speed, rather than stalking, to catch its prey. The bare pads on its feet are grooved, thus giving the cheetah better control when running.

An average cheetah is about four feet long and can weight 88 to 157 pounds. It has a darkly spotted, tawny to fawn coat of coarse fur. The feel of the fur and the look of the feet resemble the dog family. Like lions and other big cats, the cheetah greets another of its kind by rubbing cheeks.

At one time in the far past, cheetahs were trained to hunt gazelles and antelopes in Assyria and Egypt. The eastern conqueror Kublai Khan is said to have kept a thousand cheetahs just for hunting. In a record of an Egyptian festival procession (c. third century B.C.E.) honoring Dionysus (Greek god of wine, the woodlands, pleasure, and rebirth) there were lions, cheetahs, and leopards.

---

3.   However, this speed can only be maintained for a few hundred yards.

©Mark Newman / International Stock

Cheetahs (*Acinonyx jubatus*) in the wild

Chinese Desert Cat

Also known as the pale desert cat (*Felis bieti*), this animal ranges inside an area encompassed by the outer borders of China, eastern Tibet, and Mongolia. Although this creature is called a desert cat, it roams the steppes and forested mountains. Ferocious, hardy, and agile, this cat lives a secluded life.

A rather large, yellowish gray cat, this feline is about thirty-three inches long, with the tail alone being over thirteen inches. This cat is darker on the back and sides, with stripes extending to the flanks. The fur grows longer in the cold winter months.

Clouded leopard (*Panthera nebulosa*)

Clouded Leopard

An endangered species, the small clouded leopard (*Panthera nebulosa*) lives in southeast Asia, from the Himalayas to Formosa, including southern China, Indochina, Nepal, and Burma. In Borneo and Sumatra it is called Rimoau-Dahan.[4] It can be over a yard in length, with its yellowish coat marked with wide, dark disks of a dark blue-gray to an almost black. The upper canines grow to a length relatively greater than those of any other feline, resembling those of the ancient saber-toothed tiger.

This leopard lives in forests and is a remarkable climber. In its native habitat, it prefers hunting at night.

Cougar

The cougar (*Felis concolor*), also known as puma and mountain lion, is almost as big as a leopard. Found in North America, the cougar is a formidable hunter. The pumas of South America are much smaller. It can adapt to most terrains and conditions and is a strong hunter, although it seldom hunts humans. The

---

4. Some believe this name translates as "the tiger with a fox's tail," a name derived from its thick, wooly tail, while others think it means "tree-tiger."

cougar is an excellent climber, whether of trees or rocks, and has a wide hunting range.

The muscled body can average sixty-three inches with a thirty-three-inch tail. Males often weigh up to 185 pounds. The head is relatively small in comparison to the body, and is rather bullet-shaped and rounded at the face; its ears are small. The rear legs are longer than those in front. Its coat can be almost any shade of brown, with the muzzle and tail-tip black; some of the facial points and the underbelly are white.

For centuries there have been reports out of western Mexico of a species of large, long-legged felines called the onza, which is similar but not identical to the puma. In 1986 the existence of the onza was confirmed.

Fishing Cat

The fishing cat (*Felis viverrinus*) is a small, stocky feline who feeds off fish, crustaceans, mollusks, and water snakes. It weighs about twenty-five pounds and has a large, broad skull. Its short, coarse coat is typically grayish brown with dark spots and longitudinal stripes. The front feet are webbed, and the claws are not fully retractable. It will fight to the death rather than flee; one captive fishing cat got loose and killed a leopard twice its size.

The fishing cat is widely found throughout southern and southeastern Asia. It has also been discovered in such places as Sumatra, Siam, Indochina, Taiwan, Ceylon, and Nepal.

©1998 Ron Garrison / Zoological Society of San Diego

Fishing cat (*Felis viverrinus*)

Jaguar

The jaguar (*Panthera onca*) is found in Central and South America; it is known to the natives as *el tigre*. The Mayas and Aztecs considered it a very magickal animal, capable of shifting its shape in order to cause fear and kill people. They had a Jaguar God to whom they made sacrifices.

Mayan priests wore jaguar-skin tunics and headdresses representing this animal during certain rites; some of their movements during these rituals were imitations of the jaguar's stealthy movement through the jungles. The special god of the Aztec warriors, Tezcatlipoca, was often pictured as a jaguar. The Toltecs associated the jaguar with rain and thunder, which were called his "voice." His yellow skin represented the Sun. The Toltecs believed that the Sun God became a jaguar when he went underground at night.

On rare occasions, a pure black jaguar will be seen. These black cats are sometimes called panthers by the natives.

A massive cat, the jaguar has a tiger-looking coat but with black circles on the back and flanks. The head is very large, the chest deep and powerful. It can measure up to seventy-three inches in length with a thirty-inch tail. It rivals the tiger in strength and cunning. Like the tiger, the jaguar is a superb hunter in the water and has been known to kill caiman.

Jaguarondi

The jaguarondi (*Felis yagouroundi*) is found through Texas and Arizona and from Mexico to Paraguay. It is the most unfeline-looking member of the cat family and actually resembles an otter. A forest-dwelling animal, the jaguarondi prefers thick undergrowth, where it can prowl the ground during early morning and late evening to hunt rodents, birds, and small mammals.

The individual hairs of the jaguarondi are of three colors. At the root they are dark gray; this deepens to black and then becomes a light gray at the tips. This solitary animal communicates with bird-like chirps and purring. Some South American Indians keep the jaguarondi as pets to kill rodents.

Other climbing, tree-living cats of South America are the kodkod, the mountain cat, Geoffrey's cat, and the Pampas cat. Within these species alone, there may be thirty to forty or more varieties.

©1998 Ken Kelley / Zoological Society of San Diego

A jaguarondi (*Felis yagouroundi*) in captivity

Jungle Cat

The jungle cat (*Felis chaus*) can be found in the East Indies, Asia, Sri Lanka, Burma, Thailand, Israel, Iran, Afghanistan, and western China as well as northern Africa. A magnificent but shy creature, the jungle cat lives at an altitude ranging from 8,000 feet to sea level. It lives and hunts in forests, plains,

Siamese Jungle Cat (*Felis chaus fulvidina*)

and cultivated fields. Also known as the reed cat, the jungle cat may have been used by ancient Egyptians to hunt wild fowl. In fact, the jungle cat has been identified in ancient Egyptian wall paintings.

The coat color of this feline ranges from grayish yellow to reddish brown; all the shades are ticked (closely resembling the appearance of the Abyssinian), as well as the legs and tail being marked with dark stripes. It has small black plumes of fur at the tips of its ears.

Leopard

A cat with a larger area of distribution is the leopard; it lives in a variety of climates, from eastern Siberia through Baluchistan to southeast Asia.

For pure malice and savagery, the leopard (*Panthera pardus*) outdoes even the lion and tiger. The pard was another name for the leopard. The black leopard, called a panther, is fairly common in Ethiopia and the East Indies.

A graceful but deadly animal, the leopard can reach sixty inches in length and weigh 90 to 122 pounds. Its coat colors range from pale yellow and buff gray to brilliant ocher and chestnut. Black rosettes dot its coat. An accomplished stalker of its prey (including humans), the leopard also is an excellent swimmer.

In Egypt, Osiris and his priests were sometimes pictured wearing leopard skins. Initiates of the Osirian Mysteries were sometimes called scarabs, other times panthers and lions; the panther's skin was used during initiations. The goddess Nafdet was a panther who was called on for protection against snakes and scorpions.[5]

The leopard (panther) was the traditional mount of the god Dionysus in Greece; sometimes it walked beside him, sometimes he rode it, and other times it pulled his chariot. Some myths say that Dionysus was nursed by panthers as a child. His priests often wore panther skins. In the Greek language, the panther's name meant "all-beast." The words *panther* and *all-beast* also connect it with the god Pan.

In Africa, the panther (leopard) was a sacred animal to the Ibo and at times was considered to be inhabited by the souls of the dead. The Chinese said it represented bravery and intense ferocity. The Arabs called it Nimir, which means courage, boldness, and grace.

---

5. Carolyne Larrington, ed., *The Feminist Companion to Mythology.*

Lion

As the largest carnivore in Africa, the lion (*Panthera leo*) can weigh 400 to 500 pounds, be nine feet long, and stand three feet at the shoulder. The males have a thick mane around the neck, which darkens with age. The tail ends in a black tuft. A powerful body, broad face, and round ears complete the commonly known image of this feline. In the wild, the lion lives only about twelve years at most.[6]

The polygamous lion is the only truly social cat and lives in prides, consisting of a number of females and their young. A patient cat, the lion prefers to stalk prey rather than run it down.

Some ancient rulers in the Middle East trained lions for hunting. Egyptians placed portraits of lions on doors or their statues before the gates of their temples as protectors and guardians. In Egyptian art, a lion with a solar disk represented the god Ra; if shown with a crescent, it represented the god Osiris. The statues of two lions facing opposite directions symbolized the past and the future.[7] The lion's original Egyptian home was very likely in the Delta during

6. A zoo in Germany holds the record for the oldest lion—twenty-nine years of age.
7. This double-lion was a symbol of Time and was called the Lions of Yesterday and Today; Budge, *Egyptian Language*.

the time this region had similar vegetation and conditions to southern Nubia; lions also existed in the deserts on both sides of the Nile.

Male lions were usually associated with solar gods,[8] especially in Greece, Rome, and Persia, while lionesses were companions of Great Mother goddesses, often drawing their chariots. Apollo Chrysocomes (He of the Golden Locks) was a solar god connected with the lion; the lion's mane was said to represent the long hair-rays of the Sun. The lion was also associated with the Greek hero Heracles and the Hebrew Samson.[9]

In connection with the Great Mother, the lioness symbolized both maternity and the capacity for vengeance. Representations of Mother Goddesses with their guardian-companion lionesses have been found in Crete, Mycenae, Phrygia, Thrace, Syria, Lycia, Sparta, Sumeria, India, and Tibet. Lionesses aided the Great Mother in childbirth and were protectors of the dead who returned to Her earthly body.

The Egyptians believed that the lion presided over the annual Nile floods. The goddess Mut, as consort of Amun at Thebes, was both a lioness and a warrior deity; in her Theban temples she was shown wearing a lion mask. Tefnut, in her role as Sekhmet, was a lion goddess, as was Mekhit.

The lion-goddess Tefnut, top; Egyptian Lion Gods of Yesterday and Today, right

---

8. Manly P. Hall, *The Secret Teachings of All Ages.*
9. Samson was in reality the Arabic Sun god whose name was Shams-On.

Strangely enough, the Babylonians and Sumerians considered the lion to be a member of the dog family. In their literature, the lion is a metaphor for a war king or fierce deity. Stone lions guarded the temple entrances of the god Enki at Eridu and of Ishtar at Kalhu.

The zodiac signs of the Babylonians contained the Lion—or, as they called it, the Great Dog. The Egyptians and Greeks borrowed the zodiac from the Babylonians, making minor changes to suit their culture, but keeping Leo the Lion.

The Persian religion of Mithraism used a lion head surrounded with a mane of Sun rays as their emblem. One grade of their initiates was called the Lion. The Mithraic Sun god Mithras was sometimes portrayed with a lion's head and two pairs of wings.[10]

The Hindus considered the lion to be a Guardian of the North. This animal also represented strength, courage, and energy to the Chinese; they even had a lion dance during their Feast of Lanterns festival.

In England, the city of Caerleon is the "Lion's Place." Cornwall's old name, Lyonesse, means the country of the she-lion. "City of the Lion" is a translation of the name Singapore; its founder, Sri Tri Buana, built the city where he saw a lion with a white breast, red body, and black head.[11] The Lion Throne (Simhasana) of Buddhism is still sacred.

By medieval times, the image of the lion was said to have great healing magick. Doctors would prescribe that their patients carry or wear a jasper carved with a lion's image; this was supposed to cure fevers and protect against poisons. If the lion was carved on garnet, it supposedly cured all diseases and protected against all dangers during travel.[12] An engraved lion's head was said to impart strength to the wearer.[13]

10. Hall, *The Secret Teachings of All Ages.*
11. White, red, and black are the traditional colors of the Triple Goddess; these colors are called the gunas in Hinduism; Cavendish, *Legends of the World.*
12. Desautels, *The Gem Kingdom.*
13. Budge, *Amulets & Superstitions.*

There is also an Asiatic lion, an endangered species and now confined to the scrub and thorn forests of the Gir Forest National Park in Gujarat, in west-central India. Once, the Asiatic lion was found all over Asia. Hunting of this animal in the early 1900s reduced its numbers to just twelve; today that number has risen to 250.

Little Spotted Cat

Another small Central American cat, who lives only in the hottest areas, is the little spotted cat (*Felis tigrina*). Since it is known by a wide variety of names, it is possible that there are several varieties of this species.

There are also the little Mexican oncillas and the Margay cats (*Felis wiedi*) from Central America. The ocelot, Margay (an endangered species), and little spotted cats are all found in South America also.

Little spotted cat (*Felis T tigrina*)

Lynx

Two kinds of lynx inhabit Asia: the Northern Lynx and the Caracal Lynx. Although the Northern Lynx (*Felis lynx*) is also found in North America, the two are of the same species but different breeds.

To Native Americans, the lynx was a keeper of secrets and occult knowledge; a powerful and silent animal, they said it had the ability to unravel mysteries. The lynx and the bobcat always seem to be smiling in a secretive way, making one think of the expression "the cat that swallowed the canary."

The Welsh Bard Gwion in *Can Y Meirch* says that "I have been a spotted-headed cat in a forked tree," a reference to the lynx.[14]

©Ron Sanford / International Stock

Canadian lynx (*Felis lynx*) in Flathead National Forest, Montana

---

14. Robert Graves, *The White Goddess*.

Europeans during the Middle Ages had a strange belief about the lynx. It was said that its urine could harden into precious stones called Lyncurius (lynx piss) or lynx stone, sometimes identified as a carbuncle and sometimes as amber.

The Northern Lynx (*Felis lynx*) is a medium-sized wild cat. In the Western Hemisphere, it can be found from southern Canada, through the U.S., and into parts of Mexico.

This member of the cat family is yellowish brown with patches of darker brown on its coat; the fur is long and soft. It has tufted ears and a short tail tipped with black. The short tail hampers the lynx in communications, but it substitutes its long, black ear tufts.

The lynx hunts at night, using its extraordinary vision to catch rodents, birds, and deer. The lynx will attack larger animals, such as the moose and reindeer, especially in deep snow where it can move easily. Greek mythology says that the lynx had the ability to see through stone walls.

The Spanish lynx lives in remote mountainous regions down to coastal areas in southwestern Spain and Portugal. This species of lynx is now endangered because of hunting; its numbers have dwindled to less than 400.

Ocelot

In Central America, the best known of the cat family is the ocelot (*Felis pardalis*). Found from Arizona and Texas in the north to as far south as Paraguay, northern Argentina, Colombia, Ecuador, Brazil, and northern Peru, the ocelot is too unpredictable for a pet, and so far has proved untamable. Although the ocelot can live in a variety of climes, it does best in the dense forest, marshes, and jungle heat.

The ocelot's fur is a pale yellow marked with black chain-like spots. The head looks like that of a leopard in shape, but the ears are small. The ocelot averages about eighteen inches at the shoulder and weighs up to twenty-nine pounds. Able to leap from tree to tree, it hunts monkeys and birds, as well as other small mammals on the ground. It also is a competent swimmer.

Pallas Cat

Pallas cat (*Felis manul*) can be found in Russia, China, the Tibetan steppes, Mongolia, Iran, Afghanistan, and around the Caspian Sea. This animal sleeps in burrows during the day, coming out at night to hunt. It depends on its sight for hunting mouse hares and pikas in fairly open country. When the pallas cat calls its mate, the sound is similar to the scream of an owl. When it is annoyed, instead of a hiss it gives a shrill sound through its closed teeth.

The pallas cat is only slightly larger than a domestic cat, weighing about seven to eight pounds. It is around twenty-two inches long with a ten-inch tail. The broad, short head is topped with rounded, blunt ears that are set low; this enables the animal to present a minimal outline when peering over rocks or shrubs. Its fur is longer and denser than that of most wild cats, and is a yellowish brown with dark ticking; the tail is ringed with dark stripes.

Sand Cat

An example of one of the small cats is the sand cat (*Felis margarita*) found from the Sahara in Africa all the way to Baluchistan in Asia. A dweller of arid and desert regions, the sand cat hunts sand voles, jerboas, reptiles, birds, hares, and locusts. Most of its water requirement is obtained from its prey.

This small feline (about twenty inches long) has soft, dense fur, which can be in colors of pale yellow to darkish gray. The tail is striped with dark brown rings. Its face is broad and its ears large. The full cheeks have well-developed whiskers. The paws are heavily padded and feathered to protect it from burning sands.

Serval Cat

In Africa, from Algeria to the Cape of Good Hope, the *Felis serval*, or serval cat, can be found. It is less nocturnal than most small African wild cats, preying on several kinds of rats, hares, lizards, and birds. Superb swimmers, the serval cat prefers to live in forest and grasslands.

Taller and stronger than the European wild cat, the serval has a short tail and thick fur that is beige, tawny, or reddish with spots of black. Its large, long ears are tapered like the lynx, except the ends aren't pointed or have tufts. These large, oval ears are so sensitive that the serval can detect burrowing rodents, yet mobile enough to flatten in sparse cover. The tail is quite short in comparison to the body. The very agile serval can get up to thirty-two inches long and weigh as much as thirty-five pounds.

Sand cat (*Felis margarita*)

Temminck's Golden Cat

The very unusual-looking Temminck's golden cat (*Felis temmincki*) is found in southeast Asia, Nepal, Burma, Tibet, China, Indochina, Siam, Malaya, and Sumatra. C. Jacob Temminck, a Dutch naturalist, first described the species. This feline lives in woodlands and forest. Among the Asians, it is called the yellow leopard (huang poo) by the Chinese and the fire tiger by those of Burma. Since it does not climb well, the golden cat preys on a select diet of various birds and ground dwellers.

The basic background color of its coat can be a beautiful gold, yellow-brown, dark brown, red, or gray. However, it has an elaborately patterned face, black

Southern Golden Cat (*Felis temmincki temmincki*)

ears, and a plain body. A long feline (up to forty-one inches), the golden cat has only a fifteen-inch tail, which does not taper. It has a large head and short, round ears.

There are a number of other Asian wild cats: the Chinese desert cat, rusty-spotted cat, sand cat, jungle cat, marbled cat, bay cat, and the flat-headed cat.[15]

Tiger

The tiger (*Panthera tigris*) is one of the few members of the cat family that likes to swim. For brutal savagery and feats of power, the tiger easily outdoes the lion. However, the tiger is now an endangered species because of the belief that its bones have curative powers.

The tiger ranges from Sumatra to Borneo and north to Siberia. Today, the largest populations of these savage felines are in Nepal, India, Bangladesh, and Malaysia.

The tiger has a long, massive body with the tail about half the body length. The largest is the Siberian tiger, which can weigh as much as 500 pounds. The basic background color of the Bengal tiger's coat is a shade of orange to ocher, with dark stripes. Parts of the muzzle, throat, whiskers, chest, and belly are white or cream. A few purely white background tigers do exist. The Siberian tiger is also a very light or white color with black stripes.

Preferring to hunt at night, the tiger feeds on just about whatever it wishes to eat that is available. There are documented cases of tigers killing and eating crocodiles.

To the people of India, the tiger represents royalty, power, and fearlessness. In Japan, this animal symbolizes courage and warrior qualities. However, to the Chinese, where the tiger is considered Lord of the Land Animals, the mythologies are full of tiger tales. Sometimes it is pictured with wings, a symbol of its supernatural powers. It represents authority, courage, ferocity, and military might.

The most interesting application of the tiger symbol by the Chinese is in their representation of the four Elements, or directions. A white tiger is in the West and symbolizes Autumn, the Element of metal, and frightens away evil spirits and guards graves. A blue tiger is in the East, standing for plant life and Spring. In the South is a red tiger, who represents Summer and life. A black tiger symbolizes the North, Winter, and the Element of Water. In the center space is a yellow tiger, emblem of the Sun and the ruler.

---

15. Fernand Mery, *The Life, History & Magic of the Cat.*

Afterword

I hope you have enjoyed discovering all the fascinating details of felines and their magickal lives, as I did when compiling this book. The domestic cat is a marvelous creature, full of love and healing and its own kind of magick. Whatever its breed—from the non-pedigreed to those with lengthy papers—the cat has proved itself to be a wonderful, loving companion, a psychiatrist on duty at all hours, a solicitous friend and healer.

We can never presume to know why certain cats come into our lives, especially if we believe in the powers of the goddess Bast. Just before I started writing this book, we were chosen by little Valkyrie and Beowulf, but lost Finnigan to illness. We thought that the new cats, who joined Callisto, were to be the end of additions to our family for some time. We were wrong. When we discovered that three tiny kittens were to be disposed of, we couldn't say no. These feisty little furballs (whose mother was a purebred Siamese seal point) are Hocus Pocus (Pokey), Hexi, and Shadow.

Cats are delightful creatures, intelligent and unique in their approach to life and living with humans. Perhaps if more humans thought we could learn something useful from cats, the human condition might improve. I leave you with the insightful words of Fernand Mery:

> With the qualities of cleanliness, discretion, affection,
> patience, dignity, and courage that cats have,
> how many of us would be capable of being cats?

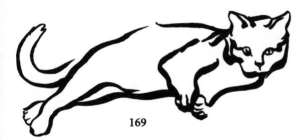

Appendix of Cat Breeds

There are more differences in breeds of cats than just the appearance. Temperaments can also differ according to the ancestry. For example, Siamese (and cats who are part Siamese) are ordinarily more outgoing and active than Persians, who are more sedate. Siamese are also more talkative than almost any other breed and are more likely to climb curtains, bookcases, or the nearest human in pursuit of some flying creature.

> There are two means of refuge from the miseries of life: music and cats.
>
> —ALBERT SCHWEITZER

Although Himalayans, Balinese, and Burmese have Siamese in their ancestry, they are not quite as vocal or active.

Abyssinians are choosy and often suddenly flighty in temperament, but can be very affectionate also. Like the Burmese, Abyssinians love to play in water, as do some Siamese, although they do not like to swim as much as the Turkish Van does. The Manx is usually a quiet, gentle cat, as are Russian Blues and other shorthairs.

Dr. Neil Todd, of the Carnivore Genetics Research Centre of Illinois, found some very interesting facts about the distribution of certain physically inherited cat traits. The ginger cat is most commonly found in a narrow band of territory reaching from London to the Mediterranean and onto the northern coast of Africa; this area corresponds to the ancient routes of traders. Scotland, Iceland, the Faroe Islands, and the Isle of Man have large numbers of nearly white cats, as does the Van area of Turkey; these lands were visited or colonized by Vikings. Except for a few isolated pockets, cats with extra toes are most common in New England, New Brunswick, and Nova Scotia; it is very probable that at one time these extra-toed cats were bred as a novelty in those areas.

If you are interested in locating a breeder of a specific breed of cat, you can contact such organizations as: American Association of Cat Enthusiasts, P.O. Box 213, Pine Brook, NJ 07058; American Cat Association, 8101 Katherine Ave., Panorama City, CA 91402; American Cat Fanciers' Association, P.O. Box 203, Point Lookout, MO 65726; Cat Fanciers' Association, 1805 Atlantic Ave., P.O. Box 1005, Manasquan, NJ 08736; Cat Fanciers' Federation, 9509 Montgomery Rd., Cincinnati, OH 45242; or The International Cat Association, P.O. Box 2684, Harlingen, TX 78551.

Coat Patterns

Bicolor
Used to describe a white cat with patches of one color or a background of another color; a two-colored cat.

Calico
A white cat with distinct patches of red and black.

Pointed
A basic, darker color on the face, ears, legs, and tail with the body usually cream, fawn, or white.

Classic Tabby
Broad markings that form bull's-eye circles on each side of the cat, surrounded by broken rings. "M" frown marks on the forehead. A long vertical stripe runs down the spine. Bracelets also ring the legs and neck.[1]

Ticked Tabby
There are no stripes or blotches, except for a dark stripe down the back. The underside is lighter and the body hairs are ticked. The face, legs, and tail have tabby stripes or rings. Ticked means that the hair has a light root and a darker tip (or vice versa), giving a grizzled look to the fur.

Tortoiseshell
Blended and indistinct patches of red and cream combined with a color such as black or chestnut. A blaze of white or red often appears on the face. Chances are 200 to one of finding a male tortoiseshell cat.

There is some evidence to the old belief that the color of a cat's coat reflects its temperament. Generally, tabby cats are the most placid, while orange males tend to be more aggressive.

---

1. The name "tabby" may have come from the Attabiah district of old Baghdad, where the Jews made a black and white watered silk. When this silk appeared in Britain, it was called "tabbi" silk. The water marks on the silk resemble the patterns on the tabby cat.

Abyssinian

The Abyssinian has a moderate triangular head with large gold or green eyes set wide apart, with pencil markings under the eyes. Its large ears are slightly pointed and tufted. The front legs are slightly longer than the back ones, and the feet are small and oval. It is medium in size and carries itself with a regal grace. A slender, finely boned cat, the Abyssinian's tail is long and tapering. It has a distinctly ticked,[2] double coat, which can come in several colors: ruddy, red, blue, and fawn. It shows a lively, active interest in its surroundings.

The Abyssinian was brought to England by soldiers in the late 1860s from the Abyssinian War. Some people think that this cat was originally part of the sacred cats of ancient Egypt. It certainly does look like ancient Egyptian bronze statues of their cats: long body, large ears, and long tail.

American Bobtail

This is a stocky, longhaired cat with a rugged appearance and a short tail. The short tail reaches halfway to the cat's hocks; sometimes the tail ends in a knot or point. This cat can be medium to large in size, muscular but not fat. The bobtail has a medium-length coat, which is non-matting, and can be in any color or pattern. The eyes are large and slightly rounded, the medium-large ears wide at the base. Its temperament is amiable and sweet.

This breed of cat began with a crossing between a seal point Siamese female and a short-tailed common tabby male. Later, Birman and Himalayan were mixed into this breed.

American Curl

The American Curl gets its name from its unusual curled ears, which result from a spontaneous mutation. Unlike the Scottish Fold, whose ears fold forward, the Curl cat's ears are erect and open, curling away from the cat's face. In fact, the ears may curl backward to at least a ninety-degree angle. Like the Scottish Folds, these cats seem to have no problems relating to the curled-back ears. It takes four to seven days for the ears on a newborn kitten to begin to curl. This curl will continue to intensify over several months.

---

2. The Abyssinian is sometimes called the hare-cat because its fur is similar in pattern to that of hares.

The head is a modified wedge, longer than it is wide. A medium-sized cat, its medium long, silky coat comes in many colors; the tail is plumed. The American Curl cat is very gentle and gregarious.

Joe and Grace Ruga of Lakewood, California, discovered a longhaired black stray with curled-back ears in 1981, which they named Shulamith. Through their efforts, the American Curl came to be recognized as a breed.

American Shorthair

This is listed as a true breed of working cat; in other words, the ordinary cat we see so frequently. Medium to large in size, this Shorthair has a short, thick, even coat that comes in a large variety of colors; the most popular color is that of the black and silver tabby. The Shorthair has an oblong head with full cheeks. The ears are slightly rounded at the tips and medium in size. It is strongly built, agile, and powerful. In the tabby patterns, an "M" can be seen on the forehead. It is larger and more powerful than the British Shorthair.

Shorthaired cats came to North America with the earliest settlers (1500s). Although they were probably brought over as pets, they likely earned their ship passage by catching rats and mice. Some people believe that there was at least one cat on board the Mayflower, which landed in 1620.

American Wirehair

Originating from a male kitten born in 1967 in Verona, New York, this breed is not well known outside North America. The guard hairs on this breed of cat are thin and bent at the ends, giving a frizzy appearance to its fur. Since every hair is bent, this makes the coat dense and springy, feeling much like lamb's wool. Even the whiskers are crimped and curly. If the fur gets wet, it may take several days for the coat to regain its crinkled, springy appearance. Its body shape is very similar to the American Shorthair, although it is often slightly smaller.

Kittens are born with tight, curly fur. It can take as long as five months for them to develop the crimped texture of the adults. The American Wirehair is noted for living long, being very playful, and having a curious nature.

Balinese

Except for its longhaired, silky coat, the Balinese cat is much like the Siamese: long, wedge-shaped head, sleek body, and almond-shaped vivid blue eyes. It has long, slim legs, dainty feet, and large ears. Like the Siamese, it comes in four basic color points: blue, chocolate, lilac, and seal; however, the coat may also be lynx point. It has long, tapering lines and longer fur than a Siamese does. An active, affectionate cat, the Balinese is quite graceful.

The Balinese cat has a Siamese ancestry. At first, when longhaired kittens appeared in litters of pedigreed Siamese, they were considered a mutation. Over the years, however, some people have come to believe this long hair is a recessive genetic characteristic. The first longhaired Siamese cat was registered in 1928. The actual Balinese breed resulted from the mating between Siamese and Angoras. They are less vocal than the Siamese.

Bengal

The Bengal has the spotted pattern, colors, and facial qualities of the Asian leopard cat. Its beautiful spotted or rosetted coat comes in yellow, buff, tan, golden, and orange, with the rosettes in black, brown, tan, chocolate, or cinnamon. Its short to medium coat is thick and soft to the touch. Bengals are divided into three color groups: leopard, snow leopard, and marble leopard.

The head is a broad wedge with full muzzle and high, pronounced cheekbones; it is small in proportion to the body. The eyes are large and set wide. The ears are small, rounded, and set far back on the head. The Bengal has a robust, long body with large paws and thick tail. Bengals generally love to play in water. Instead of hissing when annoyed, it will growl.

The Bengal originated from crossbreeding between domestic shorthair cats and the wild Asian leopard cats (*Felis bengalensis*) in the early 1960s. Although the Bengal has a wild ancestry, its personality is amiable, quick, curious, playful, and not in the least aggressive.

Birman

A sacred temple cat from Burma, and different from the Burmese, the Birman is a creature of mystery and ancient legend. It is a colorpoint cat with semi-long, silky hair (which doesn't mat like the Himalayan and Persian) and four pure white feet. It is long and stocky, with round blue eyes. The Birman's points are colored blue, chocolate, lilac, cinnamon, fawn, and seal point; the points on Birman kittens darken as they get older. Occasionally, they will be red, cream, tortoiseshell, or lynx point also. It has a broad head, full cheeks, and rounded muzzle. A long cat, the Birman has large, round paws and a ruff of fur around the neck. They are sensitive yet playful.

Legend says the Birman cats came from the Buddhist temples of Burma. The first recognition of this breed of cat came in 1925 in France.

Bombay

The Bombay is a gorgeous, sleek, jet-black cat with round, vivid gold or copper eyes. A medium-sized animal, the Bombay has short fur and a solid body. Its head is round, with chubby cheeks and a short, strong muzzle. The ears and eyes are set wide apart. The kittens of this breed have blue eyes at birth; these change to gray and then to the adult copper or gold. The Bombay is friendly, alert, and outgoing. This cat is very vocal, craves attention, and seldom stops purring.

The Bombay is a hybrid produced from crossing the Burmese and the black American Shorthair. The breed emerged in 1958 when a pure black American Shorthair was mated with a sable Burmese. Because of its resemblance to the black Indian leopard, this breed was named the Bombay.

British Shorthair

The British Shorthair is a compact, powerful cat with a broad chest and strong legs. The head is quite large, with a broad nose. The rounded muzzle is very distinctive. The eyes are also very round and quite large. The legs are powerful, the paws firm, and the tail thick at the base. The British Shorthair has a dense coat that can come in many colors, including patterns. Hardy and pliable, this cat is a good pet.

Although the British Isles are one home of the European wild cat, the British Shorthair very likely originated far to the south. Roman soldiers brought the ancestors of this cat to northern Europe and Great Britain about 2,000 years ago. In the late 1800s, cat breeders began to select the best of the non-pedigreed cats roaming the streets of Britain and developed a sturdy, friendly, and placid feline. Although these cats are bigger than most other non-pedigreed cats and are tough-looking, they are actually home-loving animals with amiable natures.

Burmese

The Burmese is a medium-sized animal with expressive eyes and a sweet expression. Its wide cheekbones taper toward a rounded chin. The rounded eyes are set well apart but slant toward the nose. Although a glossy sable brown is the original and most common color, the Burmese also comes in blue, champagne, and platinum. A very vocal cat, the Burmese is intelligent and curious.

The Burmese cat is said to have originated in Burma. A breed of brown cat lived in Burmese Buddhist temples since the fifteenth century. However, the breed was first recognized in 1936 and can be traced to a brown Oriental female named Wong Mau.

California Spangled Cat

The California Spangled Cat is medium-sized with a long, lean body, resembling a wild hunter. It has wide cheekbones, a full muzzle, and strong chin and jaws. Its eyes are medium and almond-shaped, colored in amber, brown, sand, cocoa, or gray-brown. The spotted fur is short and velvety, and somewhat longer on the tail and belly. This cat comes in several coat colors: silver, charcoal, bronze, gold, red, blue, brown, and black. Dark bars mark the top of each foreleg, and the tip of the tail is black.

Each variety of this breed of cat has nearly identical markings but can differ in color. The only exception is the variety called the Snow Leopard; this variety is born pure white and gradually develops its spots.

Although it looks like a wild cat, the Spangled Cat has no wild blood in its ancestry. This breed of cat is the result of a meticulous breeding program by Paul Casey. In the early 1970s, breeders decided to try to produce a breed of domesticated cat that looked wild but wasn't. Four other common breeds were mixed with a feral Egyptian cat and a tropical housecat from Southeast Asia. The Spangled Cat is an affectionate, active, intelligent, and very social cat.

Chartreux

This cat comes from France and is mentioned as early as 1558 by the poet Joachim du Bellay. These blue, gray, and blue-gray cats are mentioned throughout French literature. The name Chartreux is first recorded in the 1723 edition of the Universal Dictionary of Commerce.

There is a legend of the Chartreux that says these cats were brought back by monastic knights during the Crusades. They were taken to a Grenoble monastery run by the Carthusian monks, who carefully bred them to get their unique coloring.

The Chartreux is a sturdy cat with dense, medium-short, water-repellent fur. A blue-gray animal, its color shades range from ash to slate with copper to gold eyes. Its head is broad and round, with full cheeks and a small tapering muzzle. This cat is agile, intelligent, amiable, and soft-spoken.

Cornish Rex

This curly-coated, very short-haired cat is the result of a mutant recessive gene that was first noticed in cats in Cornwall, England, in 1950. The Cornish Rex has very soft, wavy, and crimped fur, with few guard hairs. The fur is so fine that this cat is susceptible to the cold. The coat of this cat can be solid, parti-color, bicolor, smoke, shaded, and tabby. The whiskers are also crinkly and can be very fragile.

A long, slender cat, it has dainty feet, a small, narrow head, and large eyes, which can be several colors, even each eye a different color. Its large ears have rounded tips and fine fur. The Cornish Rex is quite friendly and agile.

The Devon Rex cats have fur that is more twisted than that of the Cornish Rex. The head of the Devon Rex is very unique; it is short and broad, with large eyes and very large, prominent ears, giving it a pixie look. Its playful character matches its mischievous looks.

Kittens of the Selkirk Rex (which appeared in 1987) don't fully develop their first curly coat until they are about ten months old; this coat is shed, and it is another two or three months before the adult coat comes in.

Cymric

The Cymric (kim-rick) gives an impression of roundness in its form. It has a round head with firm, round muzzle; a round rump and arching back; and short legs with rounded thighs. Its heavy, double coat of medium length comes in a variety of colors. The fur on the neck, abdomen, and upper legs is longer than on the rest of the body. The eyes are large and round, and this cat has no tail. The Cymric makes a good companion, as it is very affectionate and likeable.

The Cymric is actually a longhaired Manx, a shorthaired breed of cat from the Isle of Man. These cats have appeared in Manx litters as long as the Manx breed has existed. It is thought that the Vikings brought longhaired cats to the Isle of Man, where they bred with the shorthaired, tail-less local cats.

Egyptian Mau

The only natural domesticated breed of spotted cat, the Egyptian Mau is an active medium-sized animal. Its dense, silky fur can be bronze, silver, or black smoke with darker markings, with an "M" on the forehead. The head is a slightly rounded wedge and has large, pointed ears and big almond-shaped eyes. Its eyes are usually a shade of green[3] with dark lines running from the corners of the eyes like mascara.[4] The Mau are usually not fond of strangers but are very affectionate within the family. They like to talk, and some will enjoy retrieving small objects.

One legend of this breed says they descended from ancient Egyptian stock. Like the Abyssinian, the Mau certainly looks like statues and paintings of ancient Egyptian cats. It moves like a cheetah or small leopard when stalking through grass. Princess Troubetskoy brought the first specimens of this breed to the U.S. from Cairo in 1956.[5] It was not until the early 1980s that thirteen more Egyptian Maus were brought over.

Havana Brown

This cat's short fur is a rich, dark chestnut brown color, and its paw pads are pink. It has a distinctive shape to its narrow muzzle, brilliant eyes, and large ears. Medium in size, the Havana Brown has long legs and oval paws. Less vocal than the Siamese, this reserved cat is a people-oriented cat who likes affection.

The Havana Brown is the result of breeding a black Shorthair to a seal point Siamese with a chocolate gene in the early 1950s.

Himalayan

The Himalayan's large, short, heavy body resembles that of the Persian. Its long-haired fur comes in blue, lilac, chocolate, seal, red, cream, tortoiseshell, and lynx, and is a beautiful pointed coat. Originally, the Himalayan was available in only seal point and blue point. Some cat associations acknowledge solid colors of chocolate or lilac as a breed called Kashmir.

The Himalayan's head is quite broad, round, and massive, with large, round eyes and small ears. It has a full brush tail and long ear and toe tufts. A quiet, friendly cat, the Himalayan usually attaches itself to one person, and is an affectionate pet.

This cat is a hybrid cross between the Persian and the Siamese. Himalayans have been bred since the early 1930s.

---

3. The eye coloring can take up to two years to reach its brightest, but often pales with age.
4. One tradition says that Cleopatra fashioned her own eye makeup after the designs around the eyes of these cats.
5. These first Egyptian Mau were two silver females and a bronze male. In the late 1970s Jean Mill brought two spotted bronze cats to the U.S. from India; these were Indian Maus.

Japanese Bobtail

The Japanese Bobtail cat is slender with high cheekbones and a long nose. The muzzle is broad and round, the ears large and wide. Its tail is very short, mostly a pompom. The oval, slightly slanted eyes mark it as Oriental, but it doesn't resemble the Siamese. The hind legs are a little longer than those in front. The fur of the Japanese Bobtail is medium in length and silky, with little undercoat. In coloring this cat can be solid black, red and white, black and white, tortoiseshell, or a combination of red, black, and white known in Japan as Mi-Ke. It can be either long or short haired.

This bobtail cat breed is not believed to be a mutant, like the Manx is. These cats are also relatively low shedders of hair, making it possible for many people with allergies to have a Japanese Bobtail cat. It is inquisitive, very intelligent, and an extrovert.

Ancient Japanese records say that this particular breed of cat arrived in Japan with missionary Buddhist monks at least 1,000 years ago. Their place of origin was probably China or Korea.[6] Up until 1602 these bobtailed cats were guarded because they were considered so valuable. Then a plague of vermin began to destroy the silk worms. The authorities ordered that all cats had to be turned loose to help control the destructive vermin; cats could no longer be bought or sold. After that, bobtailed cats became quite common on the streets and farms of Japan. The first-known bobtailed cats in the U.S.A. were imported in 1908. In Japan this cat is considered to be a good luck charm, especially the Mi-Ke.

Javanese

The Javanese has long, silky hair, similar to that of the Balinese, but it comes in all the point colors of the Colorpoint Shorthair. There is no downy undercoat, and the tail hair forms a plume. Its body structure is very similar to the Siamese, with very large ears and almond-shaped eyes.

This breed of cat wasn't accepted by the Cat Fanciers' Association until 1987, although they have been around as long as the Balinese. New breeds have to fight long and hard to prove themselves before they will be recognized.

---

6. The book *Nihon Ryoiki* of 705 C.E. mentions the death of such a cat.

Korat

The Korat has a heart-shaped face and luminous green or amber eyes. The eyes are large and round, and the ears rounded at the tips. This medium-sized cat is dusky silver-blue with a heavy silver sheen to its coat. The fur is short and has no undercoat; because the hair of a Korat doesn't float off when touched, many people with allergies can tolerate these cats. The nose and lips are dark blue or lavender.

The Korat is an Oriental breed of cat originally from Thailand (Siam), where it is considered to be a good luck cat.[7] In its native land, the Korat is known as the *Si-Sawat* cat. *Si* is Thai for color, while *Sawat* refers to gray coat and green eyes.

The first picture of a cat believed to be the ancestor of the Korat is found in the ancient *Cat-Book Poems*, a manuscript now preserved in the Thai National Library in Bangkok. This ancient book was rescued from the Siamese city of Ayudha when it was destroyed by Burmese invaders in 1767; it is thought to have been 417 years old when it was taken. Therefore, we can assume that the Korat breed is very old indeed. The anonymous writer of the *Cat-Book Poems* wrote verses describing several breeds of cats. The description of a solid blue cat describes the Korat in accurate detail. Another ancient Thai legend says that this breed of cat was developed by two hermits.

Maine Coon

In the beginning, the Maine Coon was a working cat on farms and in households, earning its keep by hunting and killing rodents. It is a large cat (males may weigh up to eighteen pounds) with a broad chest, long flowing tail, and heavy legs. Its ears are high-set, large, and tufted, its muzzle squarish. Its thick, shaggy fur and rugged constitution help it to endure harsh climates. The fur is long, flowing, and silky, with a chest ruff and feathered tail. Its coat comes in more than twenty colors, in solid, tabby, parti-color, smoke, and shaded colors. Hardy and rugged, the Maine Coon cat is rather dignified and reserved.

This cat is noted for making an unusual chirping sound. And while it is common for this breed of cat to pick up food with its front paws, the ancestors of this cat did not interbreed with raccoons, as superstition says.

---

7. A pair of Korats given to a bride is said to ensure a good marriage.

The ancestors of this cat may have been the very first domestic cats to arrive in North America. At one time they were primarily found in the state of Maine. One story says that a sea captain, whose name was Coon, brought Persian and Angora cats to the U.S. These cats jumped ship in Maine and interbred with the local cats, thus introducing the longhair gene. This cat's habit of sleeping in small, cramped spaces is said to come from its days onboard ships. Another story is that Marie Antoinette of France sent gifts of cats to certain families in the Northeast and beginning this breed.

The Maine Coon is one of the oldest natural breeds of cats in North America and has been shown since the late 1800s in cat shows.

Manx

Like its relative the Cyric, the Manx has a round head, muzzle, and cheeks. Its front legs are shorter than the back ones, giving it a short arching back and muscular thighs. A true Manx has no tail at all. This lack of a tail is actually a serious genetic deformity.[8] The same gene that causes the lack of a tail also distorts the spine. The Manx has fewer and shorter vertebrae than the ordinary cat. Its short, dense fur comes in many colors. The Manx cat is shy, yet endearing and adjustable to surroundings.

There are no records of when this breed of cat appeared on the Isle of Man at least 400 years ago or exactly where it came from. The explanation generally accepted on Man is that these tail-less cats swam ashore at low tide after a Spanish ship from the Armada floundered on Spanish Rock in 1588. The story further goes that the Manx didn't come from Spain originally, but from some unknown area in the Middle East. Some people believe that the Manx originated in ancient Japan, arriving in Britain with Phoenician traders.

Norwegian Forest Cat

A big cat with a powerful body, the Norwegian Forest cat has a profuse ruff around its neck and a long, bushy tail. Its double, thick, long, water-repellent coat,[9] vitality, and resourcefulness have helped it survive in harsh winter climates.[10] Pressing down on the thick fur will leave an indentation. Its coat comes

---

8. A high proportion of Manx kittens are stillbirths and malformations; Roger Caras, *Cats*.
9. A thoroughly soaked Norwegian Forest cat can dry out in fifteen minutes.
10. Wild cats do not have long fur as it is a disadvantage. However, a few small cats, including the Norwegian Forest cat, evolved long fur in order to survive in harsh climates.

in many colors and it frequently has green-gold or gold eyes. The round head is quite large, with a wide forehead and oval-shaped eyes.

Known as the Skaukatt or Skogkatt in Norway, no one knows where this cat came from originally or how it got to this cold northern country. In 1930 it was recognized as the native cat of Scandinavia. This cat is mentioned in Norse mythology; in fairy tales recorded in the mid-nineteenth century, it is called a "fairy cat."

Ocicat

The Ocicat, although it reminds one of the wild ocelot, does not come from a wild breed. It originated from accidental mating between a Siamese and an Abyssinian-Siamese mix. The present name, Ocicat, comes from the two names by which this cat was first known: Accicat (for accidental) and Ocelette (because of its Ocelot-like appearance).

It is a medium to large animal with a spotted coat, which comes in blue, chocolate, cinnamon, fawn, lavender, silver, and silver versions of the other colors; the spots are dark. Although the kittens are born with spotted markings, these patterns begin to darken after about five weeks. The rear is slightly higher than the front quarters. The ears are quite large.

The Ocicat is a very athletic cat, graceful and lithe and fond of human companionship. This cat is truly unique, with a feral look without the feral temperament.

Oriental Colorpoint Shorthair and Oriental Longhair

The Oriental Shorthair is a very sleek cat with long, tapering lines and a wedge-shaped head. It has a short, glossy coat that comes in color points of red, cream, seal-lynx, chocolate-lynx, lilac-lynx, seal-tortie, chocolate-tortie, blue-cream, lilac-cream, seal tortie-lynx, chocolate tortie-lynx, blue-cream lynx, lilac-cream lynx, and cream lynx. Its almond-shaped eyes are usually blue. Its ears are quite large, and the tail is long and thin. The Colorpoint Shorthair is essentially a Siamese, but with points colored in shades different from the accepted Siamese colors. It is quite vocal, inquisitive, and active.

The Oriental Longhair is a longhaired version of the Oriental Shorthair. It has the long, silky fur of the Balinese and Javanese breeds, and comes in solids, shaded colors, tortoiseshell, smoke, and tabby. The eyes are usually green or blue.

Both breeds have the characteristic features and body structure of the Siamese and other Oriental cats.

Persian

Persians have the longest hair of any cat, equaling the fur length of the Angora.[11] The thick fur stands away from the body and forms a huge ruff around the neck, extending down between the front legs. They are a heavily boned cat with soft, round lines. Their fur comes in a rainbow of colors, and they have large, round eyes, which can be copper, blue, green, or blue-green. The Persian is very loving and friendly.

The Italian traveler Pietro della Valle (1586–1652) brought the Persian cat to Europe. According to his writings, this breed came from the province of Chorazan in Persia, sixteenth-century Iran. He wrote that the Portuguese brought Persian cats from Persia into India. Queen Victoria kept Blue Persians, thus making them very popular during the nineteenth century.

RagaMuffin

The RagaMuffin cat is quite large, with silky, non-matting fur and big, expressive oval eyes. It comes in a variety of colors, including blends and color points, and usually has blue eyes. The cheeks are round and prominent, the pointed ears a little small. Although a big cat, the RagaMuffin has a tendency to go limp when handled. This people-oriented breed is affectionate, playful, and gentle. Because of their amiable, trusting nature they are strictly indoor cats.

The origin of this breed of cat is very hazy. It was developed sometime in the 1960s. Selective breeding has given the RagaMuffin a very docile and gentle temperament, despite their size; females normally weigh from eight to twelve pounds, while males can weigh up to twenty pounds.

Ragdoll

The Ragdoll is a large cat with heavy bones and a full chest. In fact, mature males can reach up to three feet with front and back legs extended, and can weigh up to twenty pounds. Its fur is only in the traditional Siamese colors of blue, chocolate, lilac, and seal points; the fur is medium to long and thick and silky. The Ragdoll has blue eyes in many shades. Its temperament is friendly, gentle, and affectionate; these cats are noted for liking children.

---

11. Persian cats from the early 1900s had much shorter hair than those of today.

Born almost pure white, the Ragdoll's points begin developing after about a week. It takes three years for a Ragdoll kitten to reach adult size and coloring. The fur often becomes much lighter during the summer months.

In the early 1960s, Ann Baker created this breed by crossing a white Persian female to a Birman male; the kittens were mated to a Burmese. She named it the Ragdoll because of its tendency to go limp when picked up. This breed was the first to receive its own trademark.

Russian Blue

A slender, finely boned cat, the Russian Blue is a solid silver-gray blue in color, ranging from dark blue to lavender blue. The fur is so dense and plush that it stands out from the body, like the fur on seals. Some of the Russian Blues are quite large, and they all have striking eyes.[12] The long head is wedge-shaped, and the tail quite thick at the base before tapering to the end. It is a shy, sensitive, independent animal, but demonstrative. They meow and shed very little.

This breed of cat is also known as the Archangel cat. They got their name from the Russian city of Arkhangelsk (Archangel Isle), a port on the White Sea about 150 miles south of the Arctic Circle. From this port, sailors carried them into western Europe. One story says that Elizabeth I imported some of this breed of cat. The Russian Blues, as well as the Chartreux and the blue British Shorthair, nearly became extinct during World War II. Although considered good luck cats in Russia, they are becoming rare in that country.[13]

Scottish Fold

The Scottish Fold cat has a well-rounded head and prominent cheek pads, which gives its face a very rounded appearance. Its fur is short, plush, and dense, and comes in parti-colors, shadeds, smokes, solids, and tabbies. Its eyes are wide and large. A sweet, affectionate creature, this cat makes a good companion. They are tolerant of other domestic animals, including dogs.

This breed of cat originated in Scotland in 1951 on a farm near Coupar Angus, where a spontaneous mutation in farm cats produced the distinguishing feature of small, tightly forward-folded ears.[14] In most litters there are always

---

12. In England, the eyes of the Russian Blue are preferred to be a medium blue, but a deep green is most characteristic.
13. One of the most famous Russian Blues belonged to Czar Nicholas II, emperor of Russia.
14. The ears of newborn kittens of this breed are not folded down, but assume that position at about four weeks of age.

some kittens whose ears never fold. An interesting fact is that the folded ears are no more prone to infections than the ears of ordinary cats.

From the beginning, longhaired kittens appeared in Scottish Fold litters with the usual shorthaired kittens. They have small, tightly folded ears, a round face, and large, wide eyes. The eyes can be gold, copper, green, or hazel. Their fur comes in parti-colors, smokes, shadeds, solids, and tabbies. The Longhair Scottish Fold cats have the same coat colors as the Persian, except for chocolate and lilac.

Siamese

Siamese cats are easily recognized by their pointed faces, large ears, and long tail, and the darker shades of fur on the face, feet, and tail. The fur is light on the body with dark points, which come in blue, chocolate, lilac, and seal. The coat color of the Siamese is controlled by climate temperature; the colder the climate, the darker the coat. The vivid blue eyes are definitely Oriental: almond-shaped and slanting. The slender hind legs are slightly longer than those in the front. It is common for the Siamese to have extra toes; one Siamese cat was recorded as having twenty-six toes instead of the usual eighteen. This cat also has a distinctive voice and is very sociable toward humans and other Siamese cats. However, it does tend to be snobby toward non-Oriental cats.

The Siamese cat is said to have come from seventeenth-century Thailand. The Siamese is a slender, elegant cat who originated in the country once called Siam. Like the Korat, they were mentioned in the *Cat-Book Poems*. Protectors of the spiritual temples and royal homes, the Siamese were originally not permitted to be owned by commoners. The first Siamese to enter England in the early 1880s may have been gifts from the King of Siam.

The appearance of the Siamese has changed over the years through specialized breeding practices. In the early 1900s, for example, prize-winning Siamese cats had a much rounder face than they do today.

Siberian Cat

This breed of cat only arrived in the U.S. from Russia in 1990. Rare outside Russia, this breed of cat has been common there for over a thousand years. It has a big, muscular body, a large head, and firm paws. The tail is thick and bushy, and the fur long and dense; in many aspects it is similar to the Norwegian Forest cat. It is very playful, intelligent, and friendly.

The owners of Starpoint Cattery were the first to import this breed of cat. According to breeder Elizabeth Terrell (from her communications with Russian breeders), the Siberian cat is believed to be the direct descendant of Cossack cats.

Singapura

The Singapura[15] comes from Singapore. This tiny breed of cat has very large eyes and ears; males often weigh less than six pounds. Its beautiful coat has dark brown ticking on a warm ivory ground color, while its muzzle, chin, chest, and stomach are the shade of unbleached muslin. Its coat pattern is very similar to the Abyssinian, but the body type is quite different. The muzzle is broad, the nose blunt. The eyes, nose, and whisker apertures are highlighted in dark brown. The Singapura is very active, inquisitive, and alert.

This breed was first recognized in the U.S. by The International Cat Association and the Cat Fanciers Association in 1988.

Snowshoe

The Snowshoe is a medium to large cat with a muscular, heavily built body. The head is broad and round, the cheeks full. It is a Siamese color-pointed (blue or seal points) cat with Himalayan coat coloring, but with white markings on the face, chest, stomach, and feet. The fur is short and silky. The bright blue eyes are surrounded by darker shades, which makes it look as if it is wearing a mask.

The kittens are born pure white. It takes two years for them to develop the darker coloring on their head, legs, and tail and their distinctive white feet. Snowshoe males are much larger than the females; they can weigh up to twelve pounds and develop prominent jowls as they mature.

The Snowshoe originated from three Siamese kittens born with white feet. Although there were misgivings about this color trait, the kittens were mated with American Shorthairs, who contributed the large, muscular build for which this breed is known. This beautiful cat can be seen in ancient Oriental paintings. This easygoing cat is extroverted, affectionate, and inquisitive.

---

15. The name *Singapura* is Malaysian for the island of Singapore.

Somali

Except for its medium length, double, and very soft coat, the Somali resembles its Abyssinian cousin. It is a medium to large animal with a ticked coat in blue, fawn, red, or ruddy colors. The head is a modified wedge, tapering to the muzzle. The ears are large and the eyes big and almond-shaped. The eyes are also outlined in darker coloring, making them very distinctive and expressive. An active cat, the Somali takes a lively interest in everything and is a good companion.

This longhaired version of the Abyssinian was created by special breeding during the 1960s.

Sphynx

At first glance, this breed of cat appears to be hairless; however, it is covered with an extremely fine down that feels like suede and has no guard hairs at all. This down comes in a variety of colors and patterns, including bicolors and tabbies. This lack of hair makes this cat vulnerable to cold weather and sunburn, and it should be considered strictly an indoor cat. Because of their lack of hair, the Sphynx has to consume more calories to maintain body temperature. In order to be comfortable, this cat requires an indoor temperature of 72 to 78 degrees and must wear a soft sweater when traveling.

Although this breed of cat is not hypoallergenic, people who are allergic to cat hair find the Sphynx easy to live with. However, if one is allergic to cat dander or saliva, this will not work.

The head is small and angular, the large ears triangular and rounded at the tips, the cheeks flat. In most of these cats, there are very short or no whiskers and eyebrows. The long-tailed body is of medium build and is thick through the abdomen. This breed of cat sweats, a unique and unusual trait among felines. The Sphynx is a very affectionate cat who easily gets along with dogs, other cats, and people.

Sphynx kittens are born with only a light covering of fur that is gradually lost as they get older. The kitten's skin is very loose and wrinkled, but gets smoother with age. The Sphynx is known for its wrinkled brow.

The Sphynx is extremely rare, with only about 800 such cats in the world today. This also makes them expensive to buy.

Tonkinese

This breed of cat has brilliant aqua eyes and mink coat. Its coat is medium in length and silky to the touch. In the U.S. this cat is sometimes called the mink cat because its short, soft fur has the same texture as that of a mink. Its colors can be blue, champagne, honey, natural, and platinum, with denser, darker colors on the mask, ears, feet, and tail. The head is a modified wedge with a blunt muzzle. The ears are wide at the base and oval at the tips; the oval eyes are wide set. Tonkinese are outgoing and good-natured.

The Tonkinese is the result of breeding between Siamese and Burmese cats in the 1960s. However, the first Tonkinese was produced in 1930 by mating a brown cat named Wong Mau to a seal point Siamese.

Turkish Angora

This medium-sized cat is long and lithe with an extremely fine, silky coat, which comes in many colors, the most popular being pure white. The fur on the neck, belly, and tail is thick, giving the tail a plume-like appearance. The rump is slightly higher than the shoulders, with the hind legs longer than those in the front. The Turkish Angora's round, slanted eyes complement its pretty face; the eyes can be sapphire blue, amber, green, or hazel. It is very athletic, intelligent, affectionate, and gentle.

The Angora cat originally came from the region surrounding the city of Angora, now called Ankara, during the sixteenth century. Early travelers of the time wrote that they could see very little difference between the Angora and Persian cats. The Turkish Angora breed of cats comes from the ancient Angora breed, which some say has the Pallas cat in its ancestry. The breed was perfected in Ankara, Turkey. In the sixteenth century, it was common for Turkish sultans to send these cats as gifts to European nobles.

The first Turkish Angora cats were pure white and were known by the name of Ankara kedi. Traditionally, they had eyes of two different colors, such as one gold and the other blue. A white cat with two blue eyes is very likely to be deaf, a genetic weakness.

Turkish Van

The Turkish Van (pronounced von) gets its name from Lake Van in western Turkey, but is actually an Armenian cat. Armenian people settled in the Lake Van region and revered this breed of cat. Two of these cats were taken from the Lake Van district to Britain in 1955. Sometimes called "swimming cats," the Van is usually not adverse to getting into water.

The Van is semi-longhaired, with no undercoat, and has distinctive Van markings on the head and tail. The basic coat color is pure white with red or auburn on the tail and around the ears. This long cat has a broad body, heavy bones, and a distinctive color pattern. The Turkish people say that the white patch on the center of the head was placed there by the thumb of Allah. The neck, belly, and tail have thicker, fine, silky hair. The wedge-shaped head tapers to the chin; the ears are long and wide at the base. Like the Turkish Angora, this cat is higher in the rump than the shoulders. The Van is highly independent yet affectionate.

Munchkin

The Munchkin is not as yet recognized as a legitimate breed, although it was first introduced to the public at Madison Square Garden in March of 1911. This unique breed of cat has fascinated many cat lovers.

Cats with short legs are not new to the scientific community. In 1944 Dr. H. E. Williams-Jones, a British veterinarian, described four generations of healthy short-legged cats. Later, in 1956, Von Max Egon Thiel of Hamburg, Germany, described a Munchkin cat he had seen in Stalingrad in 1953. After this, Munchkin cats seem to have disappeared in Europe and were virtually unknown until 1983.

In 1983, Sandra Hochenedel of Louisiana discovered a stray pregnant black cat with short legs and rescued her. About half of Blackberry's kittens had short legs. This short-leg mutation is not manmade, but a natural product of Nature.

The Munchkin cat has the full-sized body of a regular cat, but the height from the shoulder to the ground is only about six and three-fourth inches. The Munchkin's short legs are a disadvantage only for jumping to such heights as a countertop or table, according to clinical geneticist Solveig Pflueger. They run extremely well and can climb trees and curtains like any other cat. Being low to the floor, they seem to take corners better than most cats with legs of the regular length. It also makes it possible for the cat to dive under a bed at full speed without ducking. Munchkins have no particular health problems, since a cat's spine is built totally different from low-slung dogs who have spinal problems.

Munchkin cats may resemble the ferret in some of their movements, but their personality is quite charming. They take well to harness and leash and get along very well with people, dogs, and other cats. Some of them have a tendency to hide caches of small objects for future playtime.

I think they are delightfully charming members of the feline family, rather like dachshunds of the cat world. Unfortunately, the supply of Munchkin kittens is limited at this time; if you contact a breeder, expect to be put on a waiting list.

Bibliography

Abelard, Miles R. *Physicians of No Value: The Repressed Story of Ecclesiastical Flummery.* Winter Park, FL: Reality Publications, 1979.

Alderton, David. *Pockets Cats.* UK: Dorling Kindersley, 1995.

Bachofen, J. J. *Myth, Religion & Mother Right.* Edited by Joseph Campbell. Trans. Ralph Manheim. Princeton, NJ: Princeton University Press, 1992.

Baring, Anne, and Jules Cashford. *The Myth of the Goddess: Evolution of an Image.* New York, NY: Viking Arkana, 1991.

Beadle, Muriel. *The Cat.* New York, NY: Simon & Schuster, 1977.

Branston, Brian. *Gods of the North.* UK: Thames & Hudson, 1957.

Breasted, James H. *Development of Religion & Thought in Ancient Egypt.* New York, NY: Charles Scribner's Sons, 1912.

Briffault, Robert. *The Mothers.* 3 vols. New York, NY: Macmillan, 1927.

Briggs, Katherine. *Dictionary of Fairies.* UK: Allen Lane, 1976.

———. *An Encyclopedia of Fairies, Hobgoblins, Brownies, Bogies, & Other Supernatural Creatures.* New York, NY: Pantheon Books, 1976.

Brodsky, Gary. *The Mind of the Cat.* Stamford, CT: Longmeadow Press, 1990.

Bromage, B. *The Occult Arts of Ancient Egypt.* UK: Aquarian Press, 1953.

Budge, E. A. Wallis. *Egyptian Language: Easy Lessons in Egyptian Hieroglyphics.* New York, NY: Dover, 1977.

———. *Egyptian Magic.* New York, NY: Dover, 1971. Originally published 1901.

———. *The Gods of the Egyptians.* 2 vols. New York, NY: Dover, 1969. Originally published 1904.

———. *The Liturgy of Funerary Offerings.* UK: Kegan Paul, 1909.

Burnford, Sheila. *The Incredible Journey.* Boston, MA: Little, Brown & Co., 1960.

Campbell, Joseph. *The Way of the Animal Powers.* Vol. 1. UK: Alfred van der Marck, 1983.

Caras, Roger, ed. *Harper's Illustrated Handbook of Cats.* New York, NY: Harper & Row, 1985.

Cavendish, Richard. *Legends of the World.* New York, NY: Schocken Books, 1982.

Cirlot, J. E. *A Dictionary of Symbols.* New York, NY: Philosophical Library, 1962.

Clutton-Brock, Juliet. *Cats: Ancient & Modern.* Cambridge, MA: Harvard University Press, 1993.

Conway, D. J. *The Ancient & Shining Ones.* St. Paul, MN: Llewellyn Publications, 1993.

———. *Animal Magick.* St. Paul, MN: Llewellyn Publications, 1995.

———. *By Oak, Ash & Thorn: Modern Celtic Shamanism.* St. Paul, MN: Llewellyn Publications, 1995.

———. *Falcon Feather & Valkyrie Sword.* St. Paul, MN: Llewellyn Publications, 1995.

Conway, William Martin. *Dawn of Art in the Ancient World.* UK: Percivalt & Co., 1891.

Cooper, J. C. *Symbolic & Mythological Animals.* UK: Aquarian, 1992.

Crossley-Holland, Kevin, ed. *Folk Tales of the British Isles.* New York, NY: Pantheon Books, 1985.

———. *The Norse Myths.* New York, NY: Pantheon Books, 1980.

Cumont, Franz. *Oriental Religions in Roman Paganism.* New York, NY: Dover Publications, 1956. Originally published 1911.

Dale-Green, Patricia. *The Cult of the Cat.* UK: William Heinemann Co., 1963.

Davidson, H. R. Ellis. *Gods & Myths of the Viking Age.* New York, NY: Bell Publishing, 1981.

Davis, F. Hadland. *Myths & Legends of Japan.* New York, NY: Dover, 1992.

Davis, S. J. M. *The Archaeology of Animals.* UK: Batsford, 1987.

de Lys, Claudia. *The Giant Book of Superstitions.* Secaucus, NJ: Citadel Press, 1979.

Denlinger, Milo G. *The Complete Siamese Cat.* Richmond, VA: Denlinger's, 1952.

Desautels, Paul E. *The Gem Kingdom.* New York, NY: Random House, n.d.

Dowson, John. *A Classical Dictionary of Hindu Mythology.* UK: Routledge & Kegan Paul, 1950.

Drimmer, Frederick, ed. *The Illustrated Encyclopedia of Animal Life.* New York, NY: Greystone Press, 1961.

Durdin-Robertson, Lawrence. *Goddesses of Chaldea, Syria & Egypt.* Ireland: Caesara Publications, 1975.

Ehrenrich, Barbara and Deirdre English. *Witches, Midwives & Nurses: A History of Women Healers.* Old Westbury, NY: Feminist Press, 1973.

Engel, Peter and Merrit Malloy. *Old Wives' Tales.* New York, NY: St. Martin's Press, 1993.

Forbers, A. R. *Gaelic Names of Beasts, Birds, Fish, Insects, Reptiles, etc.* Edinburgh, Scotland: Oliver & Boyd, 1905.

Frankfort, Henri. *Ancient Egyptian Religion.* New York, NY: Harper & Row, Torch Books, 1961.

Frazer, James G. *The Golden Bough.* New York, NY: Macmillan, 1963.

Gates, Georgina A. *The Modern Cat: Her Mind & Manners.* New York, NY: Macmillan Co., 1928.

Gebhardt, Richard H. *The Complete Cat Book.* New York, NY: Howell Book House, 1991.

George, Demetra. *Mysteries of the Dark Moon: The Healing Power of the Dark Goddess.* San Francisco, CA: HarperCollins, 1992.

Giedion, Siegfried. *The Eternal Present: The Beginnings of Art.* New York, NY: Pantheon Books, 1962.

Gimbutas, Marija. *The Civilization of the Goddess.* San Francisco, CA: HarperCollins, 1991.

———. *The Language of the Goddess.* San Francisco, CA: HarperCollins, 1991.

Graves, Robert. *The Greek Myths.* UK: Penguin, 1961.

———. *The White Goddess.* New York, NY: Farrar, Straus & Giroux, 1981.

Gray, Louis Herbert, ed. *The Mythology of All Races.* 13 vols. Boston, MA: Marshall Jones, 1916.

Greene, David. *Your Incredible Cat.* New York, NY: Galahad Books, 1995.

Guerber, H. A. *Myths of the Norsemen From the Eddas & Sagas.* New York, NY: Dover Publications, 1992. Originally published 1909.

Hall, Manly P. *The Secret Teachings of All Ages.* Los Angelos, CA: Philosophical Research Society, 1977.

Harding, M. Esther. *Woman's Mysteries, Ancient & Modern.* New York, NY: Bantam, 1973.

Harrison, Jane Ellen. *The Religion of Ancient Greece.* UK: Archibald Constable & Co., 1905.

Harshananda, Swami. *Hindu Gods & Goddesses.* Mysore, India: Ramakrishna Ashrama, 1981.

Hastings, James, ed. *Encyclopedia of Religion & Ethics.* Edinburgh, Scotland: T & T Clark, 1912.

Hazlitt, W. Carew. *Faiths & Folklore of the British Isles.* New York, NY: Benjamin Blom, 1965.

Herodotus. *The Histories.* Trans. Aubrey de Selincourt. New York, NY: Penguin, 1954.

Hess, Eckhard H. *The Tell-Tale Eye.* New York, NY: Van Nostrand-Reinhold, 1975.

Hooke, S. H. *Babylonian & Assyrian Religion.* UK: Hutchinson, 1953.

Howey, M. Oldfield. *The Cat in Magic.* UK: Bracken Books, 1993.

Iamblichus of Chalcis. *Iamblichus on the Mysteries of the Egyptians, Chaldeans, & Assyrians.* Trans. Thomas Taylor. UK, 1821, 1895, 1968.

Jacobsen, Thorkild. *The Treasures of Darkness: A History of Mesopotamian Religion.* New Haven, CT: Yale University Press, 1976.

Janson, H. W. & Dora Jane. *The History of Art: A Survey of the Major Visual Arts from the Dawn of History to the Present Day*. Englewood Cliffs, NJ: Prentice Hall, 1962.

Jay, Roni. *Mystic Cats*. UK: Godsfield Press, 1995.

Jobes, Gertrude. *Dictionary of Mythology, Folklore & Symbols*. New York, NY: Scarecrow Press, 1962.

Johnson, Buffie. *Lady of the Beasts: Ancient Images of the Goddess & Her Sacred Animals*. San Francisco, CA: Harper & Row, 1981.

Johnson, James B. *The Mini-Atlas of Cats*. Neptune City, NJ: T. F. H. Publications, 1991.

Jung, C. G. *The Archetypes & the Collective Unconscious*. Trans. R.F.C. Hull. Princeton, NJ: Princeton University Press, 1990.

Kipling, Rudyard. *Just So Stories*. NY: Doubleday & Co., 1902.

Klingender, F. *Animals in Art & Thought to the End of the Middle Ages*. UK: Routledge & Kegan Paul, 1971.

Lamy, Lucie. *Egyptian Mysteries: New Light on Ancient Knowledge*. UK: Thames & Hudson, 1981.

Larrington, Carolyne, ed. *The Feminist Companion to Mythology*. UK: Pandora, 1992.

Levy, Gertrude R. *The Sword from the Rock*. UK: Faber & Faber, 1953.

Levy, Rachel G. *Religious Conceptions of the Stone Age & Their Influence Upon European Thought*. New York, NY: Harper & Row, 1963.

Lurker, Manfred. *The Gods & Symbols of Ancient Egypt*. UK: Thames & Hudson, 1991.

MacCulloch, J. A. *The Celtic & Scandinavian Religions*. Westport, CT: Greenwood Press, 1973.

Matthews, John, and Caitlin Matthews. *The Aquarian Guide to British & Irish Mythology*. UK: Aquarian Press, 1988.

Mellaart, James. *Catal Huyuk: A Neolithic Town in Anatolia*. New York, NY: McGraw-Hill, 1967.

———. *Excavations at Hacilar*. Edinburgh, Scotland: University of Edinburgh Press, 1970.

Mery, Fernand. *The Life, History & Magic of the Cat.* Trans. Emma Street. New York, NY: Grosset & Dunlap Publishers, 1968.

Michell, John. *Megalithomania: Artists, Antiquarians & Archaeologists at the Old Stone Monuments.* New York, NY: Cornell University Press, 1982.

Morganwg, Iolo, ed. *The Triads of Britain.* UK: Wildwood House, 1977.

Morris, Desmond. *Catlore.* New York, NY: Crown Publishers, 1987.

Moyes, Patricia. *How to Talk to Your Cat.* New York, NY: Wings Books, 1993.

Necker, Claire. *The Natural History of Cats.* New York, NY: A. S. Barnes & Co., 1970.

Neumann, Erich. *The Great Mother: An Analysis of the Archetype.* Trans. Ralph Manheim. Princeton, NJ: Princeton University Press, 1955.

Ochs, Carol. *Behind the Sex of God.* Boston, MA: Beacon Press, 1977.

Page, Michael & Ingpen, Robert. *Encyclopedia of Things That Never Were.* New York, NY: Viking, 1987.

Potter, Carole. *Knock on Wood & Other Superstitions.* New York, NY: Bonanza Books, 1983.

Potter, Stephen & Sargent, Laurens. *Pedigree.* New York, NY: Taplinger Publishing, 1974.

Radford, Edwin, and Mona A. Radford. *Encyclopaedia of Superstitions.* New York, NY: Philosophical Library, 1949.

Richardson, Emmeline. *The Etruscans.* Chicago, IL: 1964.

Ross, Anne. *Druids, Gods & Heroes.* New York, NY: Schocken Books, 1986.

———. *The Folklore of the Scottish Highlands.* New York, NY: Barnes & Noble, 1976.

Rufus, Anneli S. & Lawson, Kristan. *Goddess Sites: Europe.* San Francisco, CA: HarperCollins, 1990.

Russel, J. B. *Witchcraft in the Middle Ages.* Ithaca, NY: Cornell University Press, 1972.

Salmony, Alfred. *Antler & Tongue.* Ascona, Switzerland: Artibus Asiae, 1954.

Sillar, Frederick Cameron & Meyler, Ruth Mary. *Cats Ancient & Modern*. New York, NY: Viking Press, 1966.

Simek, Rudolf. *Dictionary of Northern Mythology*. Trans. Angela Hall. UK: D. S. Brewer, 1993.

Sjoo, Monica, and Barbara Mor. *The Great Cosmic Mother: Rediscovering the Religion of the Earth*. San Francisco, CA: Harper & Row, 1987.

Skene, W. F., trans. *The Four Ancient Books of Wales*. 2 vols. New York, NY: AMS Press, 1984–5.

Spretnak, Charlene. *Lost Goddesses of Early Greece: A Collection of Pre-Hellenic Mythology*. Boston, MA: Beacon Press, 1978.

Stephen, John Richard, ed. *The King of the Cats & Other Feline Fairy Tales*. Winchester, MA: Faber & Faber, 1993.

Stone, Merlin. *Ancient Mirrors of Womanhood: A Treasury of Goddess & Heroine Lore From Around the World*. Boston, MA: Beacon Press, 1990.

———. *When God Was a Woman*. San Diego, CA: Harcourt Brace Jovanovich, 1976.

Sturlusun, Snorri. *The Prose Edda*. Berkeley, CA: University of California Press, 1954.

Tabor, R. *The Wildlife of the Domestic Cat*. UK: Arrow Books, 1983.

Thompson, Stith. *The Folktale*. Berkeley, CA: University of California Press, 1977.

Time-Life. *Early Europe: Mysteries in Stone*. Alexandria, VA: Time-Life, 1995.

Turville-Petre, E. O. G. *Myth & Religion of the North*. Westport, CT: Greenwood Press, 1975.

Walker, Barbara G. *The Woman's Dictionary of Symbols & Sacred Objects*. San Francisco, CA: Harper & Row, 1988.

———. *The Woman's Encyclopedia of Myths & Secrets*. San Francisco, CA: Harper & Row, 1983.

Waring, Philippa. *A Dictionary of Omens & Superstitions*. New York, NY: Ballantine Books, 1978.

Weigle, Marta. *Spiders & Spinsters: Women & Mythology.* Albuquerque, NM: University of New Mexico Press, 1982.

White, Suzanne. *Suzanne White's Book of Chinese Chance.* New York, NY: M. Evans & Co., 1976.

Wilkinson, J. Gardner. *Manners & Customs of the Ancient Egyptians.* UK: John Murray, 1841.

Wolkstein, Diane, and Samuel N. Kramer. *Inanna: Queen of Heaven & Earth.* New York, NY: Harper & Row, 1983.

Wood, Gerald. *Animal Facts & Feats.* Garden City, NY: Doubleday & Co., 1972.

Yeats, William Butler, and Lady Gregory. *A Treasury of Irish Myth & Folklore.* NY: Gramercy Books, 1986. Originally published 1888.

Zeuner, F. E. *A History of Domesticated Animals.* UK: Hutchinson, 1963.

Zimmer, Heinrich. *Myths & Symbols in Indian Art & Civilization.* Princeton, NJ: Princeton University Press, 1946.

Zipes, Jack, trans. *The Complete Fairy Tales of the Brothers Grimm.* New York, NY: Bantam Books, 1992. Originally published in 1812.

Illustration Acknowledgments

All illustrations have been granted permission to be reprinted in this book by their respective sources, listed below.

Clip Art Book; 121—*2000 Early Advertising Cuts* (Dover); 122—[lower left] photo by Deb Olson, [upper right] Shelly Bartek; 124—[top] *Old-Fashioned Vignettes* (Dover), [bottom] Shelly Bartek; 126—Shelly Bartek; 128—©Rob Sanford/International Stock; 130—DeskGallery; 131—Shelly Bartek; 132—photo by Deb Weichel; 135—Shelly Bartek; 137—Shelly Bartek, DeskGallery; 138—DeskGallery; 139—Shelly Bartek; 140—Shelly Bartek; 141—Alice in Wonderland sketch by Tenniel/from Fred Gettings; 143—*2000 Early Advertising Cuts* (Dover); 144—*Victorian Spot Illustrations* (Dover); 145—Shelly Bartek; 147—Shelly Bartek, DeskGallery; 148—©Zoological Society of San Diego; 150—Shelly Bartek; 151, 152—©Mark Newman/International Stock; 153—©1998 Ron Garrison/Zoological Society of San Diego; 154—Shelly Bartek; 155—©1998 Ken Kelley/Zoological Society of San Diego; 156—©1989 Zoological Society of San Diego; 158—(Dover); 158—*The Clip Art Book*; 159—both from Budge, *The Gods of the Egyptians*; 160—*Heraldic Designs for Artists and Craftspeople*; 161—©1998 Ron Garrison/Zoological Society of San Diego; 162—©Ron Sanford/International Stock; 165—©1998 Ken Kelley/Zoological Society of San Diego; 166—©Zoological Society of San Diego; 169—Shelly Bartek; 224—Shelly Bartek

Index